A New Look at the Silenced Majority

Kirsten Amundsen, one of the first writers to offer an original political analysis of "the woman question" in the United States, is Associate Professor of Government at California State University, Sacramento.

Author of the best-selling **The Silenced Majority,** she has gained national and international recognition for her political reportage and lectures in recent years.

Kirsten Amundsen

A New Look at the Silenced Majority

Women and American Democracy

A SPECTRUM BOOK

Prentice-Hall, Inc., *Englewood Cliffs, N.J. 07632*

Library of Congress Cataloging in Publication Data

AMUNDSEN, KIRSTEN.
    A new look at the silenced majority.

    (A Spectrum Book)
    Edition of 1971 published under title: The silenced majority.
    Includes bibliographical references and index.
    1. Women—United States.   2. Women's rights—United States.   I. Title.
HQ1426.A68 1977   301.41'2'0973   76-58411
ISBN 0-13-615336-4
ISBN 0-13-615328-3 pbk.

The table on page 94 is used by permission of *Media Report to Women*, 3306 Ross Place, N.W., Washington, D.C. 20008.

A Spectrum Book

10 9 8 7 6 5 4 3 2 1

Printed in the United States of America

Prentice-Hall International, Inc., *London*
Prentice-Hall of Australia Pty. Limited, *Sydney*
Prentice-Hall of Canada, Ltd., *Toronto*
Prentice-Hall of India Private Limited, *New Delhi*
Prentice-Hall of Japan, Inc., *Tokyo*
Prentice-Hall of Southeast Asia Pte. Ltd., *Singapore*
Whitehall Books Limited, *Wellington, New Zealand*

To Sven and Eric

Contents

Preface

As I first set out to write *The Silenced Majority* in 1970, the step-by-step exploration of the full dimensions and impact of sexism presented something of a shock. Most all readers commented on the dramatic contrast drawn between the popular images of American women and the harsh realities of life facing them even today. Not only was insult and injury done to every individual member of this majority group; the toll was found to be a heavy one in the political arena as well. The conclusion was inescapable: our pervasive patterns of sexual discrimination and our ideology of sexism will have to be attacked and eliminated in order for genuine social and political democracy to come into existence in the United States.

Now—after numerous printings of the book and several years of feminist activity and recorded progress—I have been asked to review the data and make the necessary reinterpretations for a new edition. And the road to discovery has again been a fascinating one—and yet a profoundly disturbing one as well.

As some colleagues and many friends in the movement suspect, there is no reason to change the key conclusions arrived at in the *The Silenced Majority*. What the new findings reveal is the superficiality and token nature of the changes that have come about in recent years. *More* than the formality of Equal Rights legislation, *more* than the sterile promises of Affirmative Action is required for women to finally get their due, for genuine equality of opportunity to be created for the female half of this nation. There are yet lessons to be learned, both for active feminists and their growing number of sympathizers.

A new analysis of the road traveled and the very halting progress made may help us maintain the focus on what remains the key problem: power—and women's lack of the same. One conviction remains: for the millions of women and men who have been touched by the ideas and aspirations of feminism, there is no turning back.

Acknowledgments

The stimulus for this book came, of course, from the sisters involved in the fight for women's liberation and the many excellent writings and illuminating discussions I've been exposed to since the movement "took off" a decade ago. Though my own involvement with the issue is of long standing, it was the renewed political activities on the part of feminists that spurred me on in this project. The virtually total neglect on the part of my discipline, political science, in regard to the "woman question" in America provided whatever additional motivation was needed.

Specifically, thanks are owed to Tina Said and Joy Andrew Huelster who assited me in digging out the essential data. Typing of the manuscript was done by Meredith Crown and Susan Garbini. All four offered valuable criticism for parts of the book.

I owe thanks as well to friends and to my sons, who bore with my one-track mind in this period and helped restore my balance and sense of humor with their sympathetic attention and occasional salty remarks!

A New Look at the Silenced Majority

one

The American Woman
myth and reality

There is a familiar image of the American woman. We know it from private jokes and public commentary, from the popular magazines and the daily press, from Hollywood comedies and TV series. And we know it, above all, from advertising, in each of the media and in all possible variations.

The American woman, in this widely accepted folklore, is quite a remarkable creature. Young—or at least youngish, pretty, slender, and stylish, she spends a great deal of her time just making herself or keeping herself attractive for the man—or men—in her life. If she isn't busy changing her hair color or hairdo to catch or keep her man, she may be found tending to the vitally important tasks of keeping her skin soft, her figure slim, or her body from having any but the nicest, most enticing odor. Her main problem in life is pleasing the American man and he, in his benevolence, provides her with all the leisure and affluence to make such narcissism and comfort possible. While he is out there plugging away the usual eight hours at the office—or sometimes in a manly construction activity—his woman can spend her time at luncheons or coffee-klatches, in dress shops or at the hairdresser's, or, of course, lounging in front of the TV set.

As a homemaker or mother, the American woman is no less astounding. Her house, invariably in suburban rambler or two-story colonial style, is both attractive and immaculately kept. Her floors shine, mirrorlike, from the application of the latest finds in instant waxes; her carpets are as plush and soft as they are spotless; her kitchen is as gleaming as it is well ordered and studded with appliances and gadgets. Her kids, the darling little mischiefs, may be around to mess it all up a bit, it is true. But with efficient use of the new superaids for housekeeping and cleaning, the responsibilities of motherhood and homemaking are made as easy as they are gratifying.

The American woman, according to the Madison Avenue stereotype, comes across as a very lucky being indeed. Loved, protected, indulged, she is safe from the vagaries and challenges of the cold, cruel world out there. She does have duties, of course, but they are all of the pleasant, feminine kind. For her, the problem is not to explore, to compete, to survive in an environment of constant turmoil and bewildering change; she is simply to remain a woman or to become even more of one to the satisfaction of the man or men in her life.

There is, we must admit, a companion image of this most fortunate and endearing representative of the species. It is that of the American woman as a scheming, grasping, selfish female, hoarding most of the wealth of this country. This view is held by a good number of the "locker room" boys, but expressed by many, many more in "men's" jokes, in half-serious conversations, and in dead-serious attempts to discredit the challenges of feminists. Women own this country, it is said. They have attained great wealth and power not through their own work and accomplishments, but by cleverly exploiting the grossly unfair divorce laws or by merely surviving their hard-pressed, overworked mates. In marriage, in the courts, in the social environment in general, the American woman knows how to hold her own and get her way. Manipulating, coy, and bitchy, she can outmaneuver the all-American boy, the poor clod, almost any time she sets her mind to it. She has to be guarded against, this formidable creature—she must not be allowed to take all of the reins. The problem with the American woman, in the minds of millions of resentful, put-upon men, is that "She has it too good!"

These two common visions intermingle at times, testifying to a truly disturbing degree of confusion and irrationality concerning woman's role. Eve the darling wife and mother, embodying all the proper and appealing feminine traits, can suddenly become Eve the bitch, the coy and cold manipulator, the overbearing ruler of home, hearth, and country. The preferred stereotype, the devoted homemaker, is on occasion seen as drab, harassed, and ailing; but this condition is presumably a temporary one, to be quickly and easily relieved by use of the proper products, benefits of Madison Avenue and the ever-providing husband. Depending on their mood or the issue at hand, American men—and women, too—switch from one view to the other; but in the most widely shared conception of the role of women and the nature of sex relations in the United States, the underlying assumption is that the American woman is the one who is better off—she has most of the advantages, rightly or wrongly.

To be sure, *men, too,* can be slighted and maligned in their stereotyped portrayals in the mass media. In television commercials and situation comedies, in particular, the American man is often portrayed as a naive and clumsy dependent of the female of the species. For status, for sex, for services, or for comfort he will turn to women, ever to women, albeit of very different types. His need to win the approval of and/or to capture women seemingly drives him to buy ever bigger and better cars and a multitude of questionable items to project a "masculine" image. It must be kept in mind that stereotypes generally serve the purpose of manipulation. In advertising the goal is obviously to promote consumerism and for that purpose the present insecurity and tension of sex relations in America serve eminently well. What could better promote an incessant drive for status and affluence than perpetual and not-so-subtle suggestions that women are both desirable and materialistic, demanding and fickle? To have them love him and to keep them in the style conveyed by the media as acceptable, a man will have to achieve a great deal indeed. His resentment of this plight is not likely to lessen if the woman for whom all this is being done turns out to be at times less than totally exciting and satisfying. And if she turns out to be among the ungrateful ones and claims a life of her own and a need for some privacy and independent achievement in the midst of this suffocating attention and service to her "feminine" needs, then his resentment may quickly turn to anger—a puzzled anger, perhaps—that anyone who has it *that good* shouldn't just gracefully accept the role so generously assigned her.

Women at work, women trying to make careers for themselves in fields still considered "male preserves," are conspicuously caught in the "damned if you do and damned if you don't" vise created by this attitude. If they are vital and assertive, Alice Rossi points out, they will be rejected as "aggressive bitches out to castrate men." Yet, if they are quiet and unassuming, they will be rejected as "unlikely to amount to much."[1] Sweetness-and-light talk, flattery, and unending gratitude to male bosses and colleagues will ease their acceptance into the field, but then they find that they are rejected for promotion because they lack ambition and drive!

Most have learned to play the game. Withdrawal from competition, an often-faked acceptance, and behind-the-scenes fuming are common responses among women. And men, as a consequence, may continue to pat themselves on the back for being friends and protectors of the "proper" women. Just as they are the rightful and righteous defenders of male prerogatives against the masculinized, castrating females who dare to persist in their attacks on male bastions.

No wonder, then, that there was shock and anger in this land as increasing numbers of women came to voice loud and bitter complaints! The rebirth of feminist insurgency in the late sixties and seventies met with a predictably poor reception in most circles. As "Women's Liberation" hit the scene, it immediately captured the attention of both the media and the larger public—with a vengeance! The first new stirrings in the ranks of females since the days of the suffragettes were received with nothing but scorn and consternation in the initial phase of the movement. Today—as sexual discrimination is incontrovertibly demonstrated and hundreds of thousands of women join women's rights groups—the cause, as well as the movement, is close to attaining legitimacy. It is to be noted, however, that even by the late seventies there was resentment and resistance on the part of a great many men as feminist demands and programs edged a little closer to their own territories. Again, the stereotyped images of the American woman get in the way of a genuine understanding of the problem. Half a century ago it was none other than Sigmund Freud who gave voice to the confusion and anger felt by his fellows: "What does woman want? Dear

[1]Alice S. Rossi, "Job Discrimination and What Women Can Do About It," *Atlantic Monthly*, March 1970, pp. 90–102.

God, what does she want?" His exasperated cry is still echoed by millions of Americans. Now that she has the vote and Affirmative Action,[2] too, what does she want indeed?

The best possible testimony to the power of the images created by the media is the fact that only a handful of social observers could point to signs of disturbances and dissatisfactions among American women until very recently. Until the wave of feminism swept in on the shores of America—nearly half a century after the original suffragettes won the big prize and retired from the bitter and brutal struggle—commentaries on the social and economic inequities affecting women were few and far between. Perceptive and penetrating analyses like Helen Hacker's "Women as a Minority Group"[3] and Alice Rossi's "Inequality Between the Sexes"[4] were largely ignored. It was the angry and devastating exposé of the Madison Avenue-fostered housewife syndrome, Betty Friedan's *The Feminine Mystique*,[5] that opened the way for a new dialogue on the important and neglected topic of woman's place and woman's rights in American society.

The response of women readers to *The Feminine Mystique* was a telling one. Despite the largely negative reviews by critics, nearly all of them male, the book made the best-seller list shortly after it hit the bookstores in the fall of 1963 and has gone through several printings since. Betty Friedan wrote primarily about and for the middle- and upper-middle-class housewife with a college background, and there can be no question that she reached her audience. In these circles, her name was soon a household word. Deeply resented, hotly debated, and fiercely mocked though her thesis was, it nevertheless exerted a fascination that can only be explained by its exposure of issues that touched the raw nerves and guts of both women and men.

The prevalent image of the happy, fulfilled, and secure housewife is bunk—pure bunk, said Betty Friedan. The American

---

[2] Affirmative Action aims at ensuring equal treatment and opportunities in hiring and promotion of women and minorities in all federally assisted programs. Made possible by Executive Orders 11375 (President Johnson) and 11478 (President Nixon) and the Equal Opportunity Act of 1972, the policy has brought but few and minor changes for women—as will be documented later.

[3] Helen Hacker, "Women as a Minority Group," *Social Forces*, no. 3 (1951).

[4] Alice S. Rossi, "Inequality Between the Sexes," in R. J. Lifton, ed., *The Woman in America* (Boston: Houghton Mifflin, 1964), pp. 106–19.

[5] Betty Friedan, *The Feminine Mystique* (New York: Dell, 1963).

woman is instead cajoled, manipulated, and brainwashed into accepting the role of wife and mother as the only possible and proper outlet for her talents and energies. Stifled, bored, and frustrated, she eventually takes refuge in daydreaming, drinking, and neurotic activity of various kinds, unconscious that there may be genuine alternatives to spending one's days by the kitchen sink and stove.

Since Friedan's trailblazing inquiry into the happy housewife myth, publication of new works and of data gathered by official agencies, particularly the Woman's Bureau of the U.S. Department of Labor, have brought to the fore facts that profoundly challenge the stereotyped images of American women. As the new feminism began to surface in the late sixties, it became clear that this cherished folklore was destined to be shattered beyond repair. The data were too overwhelming, the offense too obvious, and the injury too grave for the myth to persist, no matter what the attempts of the advertising industry or the media in general.

What the current literature reveals is that the life situation of a near-majority of American women bears virtually no resemblance to the images so dear to Madison Avenue. These stereotypes are totally unrealistic, new feminists point out. Worse, they are hypocritical and dishonest and do grave damage both to the feminist cause and to the psyches of individual women. Attention must be paid to the stark and bleak realities confronting tens of millions of American women today. Attention must be paid to the injustice, to the frustrations, to the limitations imposed on women generally —which thereby affect the very quality of life in this society.

There is an urgency in this claim that, given its exclusive focus, leads many to question its validity today. But what is being discussed *is,* after all, a long-overdue redress of a major injustice against half of our people and the updating and change of images that control and betray reality. To make this claim is not to suggest that men in this society are generally subject to fair and decent treatment either on the job market, in political life, or in the media. The existence of poverty among roughly one-fifth of Americans, male and female, and the lack of economic security and poverty of social services for tens of millions of Americans in the labor force all give evidence of a socioeconomic system that permits serious inequities and patterns of exploitation to affect large groups within its population. The point to be made here, however, is that women *by themselves* constitute just such an exploited group, by far the largest and, as will be shown, the most unfairly treated. Yet—and equally striking—there is far less recognition of the true socioeconomic and political situation of women than there is of the position of other "out-groups" in American society.

Poverty in America has been exposed; the problem of racial minorities is being explored; the frustrations and insecurities of male workers, both of the blue-collar and white-collar variety, have also been given reasonably sympathetic and thorough treatment. But women's status, women's opportunities, and women's share of power in this democracy are but rarely the subject of serious discussions. The very suggestion that this presents a problem is all too often met with consternation and ridicule by both laymen and scholars. We will suggest, however, that the nature, dimensions, and consequences of this problem have an impact on our daily lives that is as misperceived as it is formidable. It is of the utmost importance, therefore, that it be explored and that it be *named*. Then, and only then, can we attend to the social problems both sexes have in common within the framework of a group or class analysis.

Beyond the Stereotypes

To a social analyst, the primary task ahead must be to explode the myths shrouding our perception of the realities of life for the majority of American women. Their supposed affluence and ease of life, their protected status, their power, their sexual inferiority and "penis envy" are but some of the common misconceptions that have to come under scrutiny. The most unsparing look must be cast at what *is* known and at what *may be* inherent and unchangeable in the situation and in the nature of women. Where a myth is hollow it must be exposed as such; where a stereotype betrays the truth it must be discarded. Be the commitment an ideological or an intellectual one, the problem at hand requires a systematic and relentless exposition of the facts of the situation.

Immediately, it is the invidious and shallow portrayals of women in the media that call for our attention: woman as sexpot, woman as helpmate, woman as ever the object of man's desires and of his protective and indulgent care. How does this perception hold up

under the harsh glare of reality? To what extent, if any, does it
conform to the truth? Let us take but a brief look at the data
coming our way at this time, which suggest that reality is radically
different from the myth.

First of all it must be recognized that women in America are no
longer primarily housewives. In fact, nearly 37 million adult
women were at work in 1975, constituting about 40 percent of our
adult work force.[6] Fifty-nine percent of these women earn salaries
of less than $7,000 yearly; 28 percent, nearly 10 million, have to
make do on less than $5,000 yearly. Less than 3 percent have in-
comes of $15,000 or over yearly.

And what is life really like for these tens of millions of women
whose very existence challenges the common vision of American
womanhood? Could it be that a majority of them work for pleasure,
and not out of necessity? Are their strikingly low incomes used
mainly to supplement that of the head of the family? Might they be
motivated to take a job simply out of desire for a few extra comforts
and luxuries and possibly, also, because they have too much free
time on their hands?

No. We find that about 6.4 million of the married working
women have husbands who earn less than $7,000 yearly, and over
half of these have children of school age or under at home. Work
for them is a compelling necessity. For the single female workers,
about 7 million in all, it is almost without exception the need to earn
a living that drives them into the job market. In addition, nearly 7
million are widowed, divorced, or separated, and the incomes
earned by them are needed not just to support themselves, but very
often their families as well. Startlingly, more than 2.3 million of
these working women family heads fall in the category of the poor
or low-income levels in the United States. And among them, they
have more than 5.3 million children to support.[7]

Women who work out of necessity, women who work for
compelling economic and *not* frivolous or "selfish" reasons, number,
then, more than 20 million in the contemporary United States. We

[6]Data pertaining to women in the labor force are from the U.S. Bureau of the
Census and the U.S. Department of Labor, Women's Bureau.
[7]The poverty threshold (or low-income level, as administration spokesmen prefer to term it) is updated every year to reflect changes in the Consumer Price Index.
In 1974 it was $5,038 for a nonfarm family of four; in 1975, $5,050 for the same.

need not inquire much further into the reasons why the remaining millions are on the job market. In 1974, some 13.5 million mothers of children under age eighteen were either working or looking for work. More than half of these cited economic necessity as the main reason for seeking employment outside the home.[8]

We must ask then, how do the lives of these women—the majority of working women—who clearly have to work to lift themselves and their families out of the lowest income levels—conform to the stereotyped images of American feminity in the media?

If they are women with children at home, as more than half of them are, the comforts, the leisure, and the self-indulgence supposedly typical of the American woman will be largely unknown to them except through the pictures flashed on TV screens or brandished in newspaper and magazine ads. What they experience in their everyday existence is unending toil and frequent deprivation, not just of the luxuries, but some of the basics of a comfortable life in contemporary society. They are likely to live in substandard housing units—cramped, cluttered, and often poorly furnished. The television set will be there, no doubt, and so will the refrigerator, and, in all likelihood, the washing machine. But the other amenities of the "typical" American life will be gone: no plush carpeting, no gleaming, smart tile floors, no heavy, luxurious draperies, and no superappliances and gadgets to make housework a breeze and cooking a pleasure. The dingy little apartment, the run-down old house, or the flimsily built tract home contains little to give visual pleasure or to offer genuine comfort. It is, instead, bleak to look at and hard to keep up, adding to the strain of the invariable and tiring hours of housework awaiting these millions of women as they arrive home from their eight-hour-a-day jobs in shops, in the fields, in factories, offices, or laundry services.

At least 7 million American mothers with school-age children or children under school age work outside the home for reasons of economic necessity. Seven million at least lead lives that totally belie the vision of America as a woman's paradise, that belie the very American dream.

And what about the rest? What about the remaining and larger

[8]Elizabeth Waldman, "Children of Working Mothers," *Monthly Labor Review,* January 1975, pp. 64-67.

portion of the 25 million who simply have to be on the job market?

A little under 3 percent are well enough off, as we know, with yearly incomes of $15,000 or more. A little more than 1 million women are to be found in that fortunate class—compared to nearly 27 million men. It is to be noted that median annual earnings for married women in the labor market in 1974 were as low as $4,524. Where the husband is at work, this income is, of course, supplemental and *might* then be used for amenities and luxuries of the kind presumed to exist in every American home.

Yet, as any average American will recognize, even an income of about $12,000 to $15,000 does not connote real affluence in the seventies. There are the questions of insurance, of medical and dental bills, of college education for the kids—just to mention a few of the items that inexplicably seem to drain the budget of middle-class Americans. Let it be remembered that most of the married working women we are concerned with here are struggling to make do with family budgets of well *under* $15,000 per year. Not an easy job, that. Hardly one that allows for the self-indulgence, the pampering, and the superior comforts supposedly available to the American woman.

For all these working women with families to maintain, all 25.1 million (with the exception of the less than 1 percent lucky enough to have household help), the daily existence is characterized by work, duties, errands, and worries: an endless and exhausting round of activities that, while for many preferable to the stay-at-home life, leaves them with little time and less energy for the pleasantries, the fun, the self-indulgence coming their way in Madison Avenue's vision of the life of the American woman. It is toil, pure and simple, for the great majority. Research conducted in recent years has found that working wives average 68 working hours weekly,[9] all of that for very little pay and, all too often, precious little appreciation.

But we have only begun. We have not even looked at the millions of women who find themselves both without jobs and without husbands in our society today. Deprived of the minimal security and dignity that either work or marriage might offer, they find them-

---

[9] According to a study of housewives in Syracuse, N.Y., quoted in *Sheryn's Nifty Newsletter*, 1, no. 1 (May 1970): 1. Also, Chase Manhattan Bank estimates a woman's *overall* work week to be 99.61 hours.

selves prey to the prejudices and high-handed manipulation of the welfare establishment. Over three-quarters of welfare recipients in major cities are women. They receive welfare payments largely through the Aid to Dependent Children programs and, with too few exceptions, in these programs the rule is that a woman may not get her allowance if a man can be found to share the sorry premises inhabited by her and her children. If you are a woman and you are poor, as are millions of women today, you are supposed to do without sex as well as without comfort, security, and privacy!

The American woman is, then, both misperceived and maligned in the cliché-ridden views conjured up by the media. Underpaid, overworked, and often left with the main responsibility and toil of rearing a family, she is anything but the secure and sheltered, pleased and pampered little doll winking at you from underneath triple nylon lashes on the TV screen. Being a woman in this society at this point in time means having to deal with all of the risks, all of the challenges, and all of the responsibilities supposed to be the man's province. Moreover, it means taking upon oneself "woman's work." The only difference is that for the work women do, they will be paid less and they will advance far more slowly, if at all, *and* they will be virtually closed out of a number of professions—the highest-paying ones and the ones carrying the greatest status.

It is this situation, the deteriorating condition of women in America, together with the increasing spread of egalitarian ideas, that has led to the resurgence of feminism in the seventies. What is now demanded is an end to the domination and exploitation of 53 percent of the citizens of this democracy. What is sought is a greater measure of equality, an opening up of opportunities, a widening of options for women. What may be achieved, it is suggested, will be a new life style for both women and men, an upgrading of the quality of life in the society in general, on the social, economic, and political levels.

It is the thesis of this book that whether one's focus is on the false and demeaning stereotypes, on the inequities of the job market and in educational institutions, or on the numerous norms and habits limiting the choices of women everywhere, one will eventually have to deal with political structures and with representation within these same structures. The relationship between the sexes in America is most likely to be changed through political action, as are the relationships between the races and between different classes or strata within the society. It is through politics, after all, that one gets the rules and regulations, the important legislation that determines wages and working conditions, that guarantees access and opportunities, and that provides for the necessary services enabling women as well as men to fully develop and utilize their talents and skills. It is also, ultimately, politics that will change institutions and the social conditioning structuring both the male and female personality in this society. And it is mainly through politics that one can hope to rebuild values and to change the blatantly counterfeit stereotypes of women that now get in the way of understanding and appreciating their true situation and their genuine needs.

The Real Revolution

This, it is true, is likely to be a highly controversial proposition. It will surely be contended, now as in the past, that woman's role in society and our conception of it is rooted in biological distinctions, inherent psychological traits, and social necessities. It will be said that it is simply not in woman's nature to compete on an equal basis with men in the fields of activity now dominated by the "stronger" sex, nor is it in the interests of society that she do so; that the stock figures of woman as wife, homemaker, and mother have their base in the very natural and commendable disposition of women to conform to those roles; that these are roles, moreover, that have to be performed by women for the continuance of the essential functions of the family—the breeding and rearing of the young and their orderly induction into society.

But these arguments no longer have the ring of truth in them. We must, in the first place, contend with the fact that women in America do not now enjoy, and have not for quite some time—if indeed ever—enjoyed, in perpetuity, that exclusive and protected position presumed to be theirs. At least one-half of American women have to and do work outside the home for the larger portion of their lives.

In the second place, the condition of being a woman has changed drastically, as has the life situation of all individuals, with the coming of the technological revolution. There is, for instance, the dramatic and significant improvement in standards of living, leading to standards of longevity enjoyed only by the privileged few in past centuries. The life expectancy of women in America is now seventy-six years. At the age of thirty, most American women have borne their last child; at the age of thirty-five, all of their children will be in school. Consider, then, the implications of this change: when women are relieved of the need to watch and care for their children in the daytime hours, they have some thirty-five or more adult years to look forward to. What are they to do with themselves?

The development and increased availability of oral contraceptives has introduced yet another factor into the equation. For the first time in history, women can choose for themselves when, how often, and *if* they want to become mothers. This power alone has the potential to start a veritable revolution in the relationship between the sexes. No longer does woman have to face a future of *"Kinder, Küche, und Kirche."* She may choose it, by all means, but she can also choose to have a full life as a sexual being without being confined to the traditional role of mother and homemaker. Or she may choose to relegate these experiences to a period of her life when she is emotionally, intellectually, and financially ready for them.

The novelty of these circumstances cannot be overemphasized. Until this century, the role of housewife and mother was central to a woman's experience and dominated all of her adult life, for the very simple reason that when she was finally through with bearing and rearing children she had precious few years left to live. At the same time, housework in the past required more effort and a great deal more physical energy than it does now. Quite apart from the socialization process, which, of course, precluded the choice of any other profession for a "well-adjusted" woman, how could one expect women in their forties, with little more than a decade of life ahead, to pick up the pieces of their fragmented existence and recreate themselves as career seekers, professionals, craftpersons, or artists in a world both strange and hostile to them? It is remarkable, indeed, that some of them did.

Today, however, even the most dedicated housewife is apt to be plagued by doubts, boredom, a stifling sense of frustration in contemplating all those years ahead spent doing the same menial tasks and the unimportant busy work. She will also, if she is reasonably socially aware, be bothered by the fear of having to rely on her own resources at some time in the future. More than two-thirds of American housewives end up on the job market later in life—very often out of necessity and almost always without any decent preparation for their new roles.

To say, then, that woman's place is in the home is simply to be hopelessly out of touch with the realities of life as well as the potential for change in the experiences of women in America. Although it is true that most women still see, or prefer to see, themselves in the role of mother and homemaker, this is proof of nothing else than that there is a gap between the common perceptions of the American woman and her essential characteristics and circumstances. It is a gap as wide as that splitting the generations apart, and it is every bit as portentous. It cannot be bridged, moreover, until we undergo a process of reeducation with regard to the real situation—social, economic, and political—of women in this society and with regard to their actual needs and newly found possibilities in these same areas.

How does one set about reeducating a people in something as fundamental as its views on sex relations and family life? Independent opinion wielders can contribute to some small extent, provided they have access to the media that gets the messages through to people. But for these messages to come with the frequency and in the form necessary to change fundamental values, nothing less than a broadly based and clearly focused social movement is required. For if we are to change the common image of woman in this society—"we" meaning those of both sexes committed to seeking such change—we will have to capture control of the media and of the educational institutions that are now responsible for the creation of these images. Beyond that, we will have to gain sufficient control over decision making on the governmental level to make the changes necessary for women to enjoy equal status and equal opportunities on the job market and in higher education. We will have to push through the social legislation necessary to free women for greater and more creative efforts in their chosen activities —primarily, establishment of child-care centers, provision for maternal leaves, and abolition of anti abortion laws.

Can it be done? There are doubters and there are cynics and there are gleeful satirists all ready to cast aspersions on the goals and the potential of the new feminists. But in a society that remains open, where challengers and rebels have a chance to seek and attract support for their cause, much can be achieved through the proper study and application of politics. It is one of the great anomalies of the situation of women today that so very, very few students of politics have attempted a serious analysis of their political situation and how it can be changed. That, it would seem, is a prerequisite to the transformation of values and of life styles that is so hotly desired, yet so dimly perceived, by the new feminists.

What follows is an effort to satisfy that prerequisite.

Once More an American Dilemma

The basic assumption underlying this analysis is that it is both morally indefensible and socially damaging to have a major group of citizens in a political democracy denied access to, and opportunities for, socioeconomic benefits and political power. It is morally indefensible because of our expressed commitment to the moral equality of every man and woman in our society and because of the belief widely shared among us, incessantly called upon to cover over existing inequalities, that our institutions are so arranged as to maximize opportunities for all. And it is socially damaging, first, because of the waste of skill and talent that is involved when a substantial group of citizens is systematically prevented from the development and use of their potential and, second, because pervasive discrimination on the basis of differences created by birth frequently fosters resentment and antisocial behavior in the socially inferior group to the point where the health and stability of the entire society is endangered.

Insofar as this study is based on the above assumption, it is not "objective." It is very doubtful whether any social analysis—particularly of contemporary problems—can be. Questions posed, arrangement and interpretation of data, determination of what to exclude as well as what to include are all decided on the basis of a certain predisposition to look for some facts rather than others. The view of our eminent international colleague, Gunnar Myrdal, is surely valid, that integrity and scholarship in the social sciences is best served by the explicit recognition of the analysts' own values in conjunction with a searching and profound examination of the dominant values of the society under study.[10] The task of the scholar is quite naturally lightened if he should happen to share in the latter. And so it is in the case at hand. "The American Creed," in Myrdal's phrase, that whole body of core beliefs and values shared by all Americans, is also ours[11] (see Appendix 1).

Another assumption requires clarification at this point; it is superfluous perhaps for fellow students in the social sciences, but important for many individuals outside this field. It has become a commonplace to say that we are all products of the society in which we live. What this means, in the minimal sense, is that attitudes, habits, and predispositions are socially determined. Talents and intelligence, as well as emotional proclivities, make a difference for the individual, and it *is* possible for one person to transcend some of the limitations imposed on her by both the socialization process and the social setting. *But* the differential behavior of whole groups in terms of achievements and style of life is to be explained not in terms of inherited mental, emotional, or physical characteristics, but rather in terms of their distinct social experiences from early childhood on. Consider, for instance, this example: a black male growing up in the South thirty or forty years ago was likely to act in a deferential, devious, unassertive, and coy manner, because his training and life experience made him act thus. We have seen the startling change in black youngsters since the fifties, and we know full well that there was nothing "natural" about the behavior typically exhibited by southern blacks in the past. No one can say that blacks in this society have not by now demonstrated their will to independence, their ability to assert themselves, their seriousness, and their determination to end the pervasive discrimination their race has been subjected to throughout American history. "Coy," "deferential," and "unassertive" would be most unlikely adjectives to use in describing the young black man of America today!

So it is—or so it may become—with women. The psychological characteristics held to be "typical" of women are likely to be quite simply socially determined. No one knows what "true feminity" is, or if it can, indeed, exist except in the realm of the imagination. It

[10]See Gunnar Myrdal, *An American Dilemma* (New York: Harper & Brothers, 1944).
[11]Myrdal.

is, by and large, the socialization process that is responsible for the mental sets, the emotional dispositions, and the prevalent behavior of women—just as it is for other groups. Behavior need not be biologically determined for women any more than it is for any one race. Although it is undeniably true that pregnancies and childbirth produce both psychological and physiological changes in women, these are not the kind of transformations that affect their mental and creative capabilities over the long run. The question of the "psychology of women" must therefore be taken up anew; the whole notion must be questioned and subjected to the most searching scrutiny. Only psychologists, anthropologists, and sociologists can fully examine this most abused topic, and only a few have started the reexamination so long overdue. Their findings will be discussed in the latter part of this work. Meanwhile, let it be emphasized that this investigation of the "woman question" is undertaken on the assumption that women differ from men in physical characteristics and in mental and emotional dispositions, but that only the former constitute inherent differences. As to potential, ability, or achievement in any one field, it has not yet been proven that women cannot be the equals of men. Nor that they will not—in a different social setting—aspire to become just that.

two

On Her Own
down and under

If the American woman is no longer a mere appendage to her man, socially and economically speaking; if she cannot from now on rely on consistent or sufficient support and security in her role of housewife and mother, then what *is* her actual position in American society today? If the stereotyped images of the American woman are false, then what image would conform to the true picture of the situations she now finds herself in? Is it that of woman as a full participant, a social equal, and an accepted competitor to man in the realms of education, work, and politics? Can her conspicuously sorry state as a wage earner and her relative lack of achievements in most areas of endeavor be ascribed to the fact that she has only recently chosen to take upon herself the challenges, risks, and burdens of work that were formerly relegated to men only? May her grave socioeconomic problems be due to her being a newcomer to the job market? And do we then simply have to wait for her to catch up with the American man in training, skills, and experience for these same problems to be solved?

It should be useful and it could be essential for a genuine understanding of the situation of working women in America that their positions in the stratification system of our society be correctly assessed. It may be essential, for that matter, for the comprehension of the whole "woman question." Whatever one may think about the causes and determinants of the relationship between the sexes, it is clear that the roles undertaken by women in contemporary society and the status ascribed to those roles cannot help but affect the interaction, the orientations, the emotional play between men and women. It will, at the very least, influence the form and quality of their relationship. For those who feel an urgent need for change, as well as for those who simply want to cling to the status quo, it is of crucial importance that it be known if, how, and why the 48 percent of women on the job market[1] are assigned to ranks different and distinct from those of men holding formally equivalent positions. We need not for the moment look at the complex question of ranking between men and women in the family; since most married women will be employed outside the home before retirement age, the findings concerning *women at work* might have an impact on one's evaluation of the whole social system.

It should be abundantly clear that a systematic hierarchy of social positions does exist in American society and that we treat the occupants of these positions as superior, equal, or inferior in socially important respects (see Appendix 2). But in considering a modern system of social stratification, one must pay attention to several different dimensions. It is widely believed that we no longer have the obvious and close correlation between economic inequality and differences in authority, power, and prestige that characterizes older class systems. If we are to fix the position of major groups of women in our stratification system, we must look at their rankings in terms of three crucial dimensions—class, status, and power. We must also examine what social mobility is available for women, that is, what are their actual possibilities of moving up and down the class, status, and power hierarchies.

It is quite a novel idea—so far merely hinted at in the social sciences—that women constitute social strata distinct from men occupying formally identical or similar positions in the social hierarchy. Notably, in spite of the many indications at hand that women are treated differently in all the important dimensions, neither sociology nor political science has so far found it opportune to deal with the problem of women in American society as a problem of social stratification. Women are assumed to share the fates of their men, purely and simply. Sex positions, in the classic statement, are

---

[1]According to the *Wall Street Journal* (June 29, 1969), 44 percent of all women aged sixteen and older are either employed or seeking work.

nonstratified. It is this understanding, widely shared among both sexes, that prevents a woman from viewing her lot in life as being due to her membership in a social group, a collectivity defined not just by birth but by socially determined distinctions. Women, rightly or wrongly, appear to have no consciousness of the causal connections between their life chances and the stratification system special to their society. If Americans in general are lacking in class consciousness, as is frequently decried or applauded by observers, then American women are startlingly so!

What would be the consequences for women—and for American society in its totality—were such a consciousness to evolve? At the very least, one may safely assume a greater likelihood of concerted political action to right whatever wrongs are committed against women. An increased awareness of the rights of women must, of course, be a precondition for their liberation. Any informed knowledge of systematic discrimination and exploitation of women provides the additional crucial condition of a context in which a coherent system of demands and a strategy to implement them can be developed.

As to the *rights* of women to participate fully in all areas of life in America, there is a great deal of ambiguity in the views found within both sexes. On one idea, however, we find general agreement. Every American should have a chance to achieve the best of which he—or she—is capable. This basic belief has been a lever for social change on many an important occasion in the past. From the abolitionist movement of the nineteenth century to the labor movement of the twentieth, Americans have vigorously fought for and won rights denied them—*unjustly* denied them—on the basis of the almost universally expressed belief in justice and equality of opportunity in this society. Today there is still a disturbingly wide gap between commitment in theory and practice. But there can be little doubt that the *ideal* continues to inspire and to periodically propel disadvantaged groups into action to shorten this social lag. We have seen the most dramatic and recent example of its power in the struggle of blacks to achieve what has long been their due according to the American creed.

Whether or not the majority of women believe themselves able and entitled to share with men all of the burdens, risks, and opportunities of wage earners at this point in time is no longer of material importance. *Morally*, at least, they consider themselves as individuals to be of equal worth. Politically, they have also sought and won the right to full participation and representation, and one may assume, when such a basic value has found institutional expression throughout half a century, it has by now been internalized by a good many members of the society affected by it. Briefly, what is significant here is that the ground *has* been prepared, ideologically speaking, for a profound and powerful revolt against serious and systematic injustices against women in the economic, social, and political realms.

Consider what might happen then if the American woman were suddenly enlightened to see that her opportunities, her benefits, and her share in the social goods of the society are likely to be a good deal less than that of the American man? That *just because* she is a woman, her life chances are not only different, but significantly reduced in terms of the whole bundle of benefits and privileges that are socially produced? What might she do, were she to come upon the discovery that she is persistently consigned to an inferior status, given less salary, and afforded fewer chances to call the shots than men no more skilled or able than she? All that at a time when she is more likely to have to go to work to support herself or to help support her family in her mature years—and all that in a country where her full moral worth, her political rights, and the ideal of equality of opportunity have long been *formally* recognized?

The Female Underclass

But first, can such gross and arbitrary injustice really be documented? All social analysts will agree that where awareness of serious inequities exists among those subject to it, solidarity and group action may follow. One must, however, have a clear view of the *systematic* nature of the injustice. Only when it can be proven to be part and parcel of the whole economic order and not merely haphazard and erratic can it lead to a determined and concerted political thrust on the part of the victims. American women, like their male fellow citizens in the 1930s, may have to free themselves of the notion that their misfortunes and maltreatment on the job market are due to nothing more serious than bad luck, typical male prejudice, or individual stupidity and arrogance among their employers. If recognition of common interests among women is to develop and further lead to organization and action on behalf of women, it will have to follow upon a serious and well-publicized analysis of our system of social stratification and of women's positions within it.

What will have to be shown, then, is whether an employed woman—a worker in a factory—with a given amount of training and experience stands to get a significantly lower wage, less opportunity for advancement, and less of a guarantee of keeping her job than a man in the same position. If that can be shown, then clearly women factory workers are relegated to a lower *economic* stratum than are men factory workers, and for no other reason than that they are born of the female sex. If, at the same time, we find that a woman factory worker enjoys less esteem on the job or in the community, is subject to more constraints, and is expected to carry heavier social burdens, then obviously women constitute a different and lower *social* stratum than men in terms of their relative status. And if a woman factory worker has less of a chance than a man factory worker to influence and determine the behavior of others and fewer opportunities to exercise control over decisions that affect her life and those of others, then she is also in a distinctly lower stratum than the man in terms of relative *power*.

These are the three crucial dimensions of social stratification in a modern society. Economics, status, and power constitute the basis for different rankings, presumably not identical, but undeniably closely related. That we should have such systematic hierarchies in our society is something of an embarrassment to democratic ideology. We are saved in our democratic faith, however, by the expectation that a person is not relegated to one rank or the other solely because he is born into it. *Social mobility* is a crucial criterion in the stratification system of a democracy. There simply has to be a possibility for individuals to move up and down the class, status, and powerful hierarchies. If members of a collectivity defined by birth are persistently and conclusively relegated to lower strata than are other members of the society, then one is faced with a flaw, a very serious flaw, in the fabric of democracy. This cannot be. When we talk about *class* in a democratic society, we view it as a temporary aggregate of individuals who happen to occupy similar social positions at a certain time. In the classic definition, *class* refers to people destined by birth to similar positions and similar life chances (see Appendix 2). But in contrast to the castelike hierarchies of older states, our system, although admittedly stratified, is characterized by a high degree of social mobility. Or so it is said.

Blacks in our society have been studied, scrutinized, and subjected to concern and sympathy for more than a decade, because our attention is now focused on their continuing, and therefore inexcusable, low rankings in the stratification system. They are at long last beginning to get the kind of opportunities and assistance that will make social mobility more than a fictional term within their group. Browns are now following in their footsteps, and American Indians are said to be not far behind. But women—constituting not a minority, but a bare majority of this nation—have so far received little or no attention from serious scholars in the field. Indeed, one might say that if the poor constitute an "invisible" America, to use Michael Harrington's compelling term,[2] then women—working women in America—make up the largest and least-known portion of that sad land. There is an abundance of data pointing out that the problem of women is identical to the problem of a minority. And there are grave indicators that their situation may best be described in the terms used to designate the least fortunate of groups in the rigid class systems of earlier times. The notion of women constituting an "under class" in American society is a startling one, to be sure. Yet it must be entertained, while still held in abeyance, as we take up the analysis of the data that by now point at least partially in that direction.

Again, our first task is to survey the current job market and see if such pervasive and trenchant differences can be discovered in the opportunities and treatment offered men and women that they can only be explained on the basis of a systematic stratification scheme. It is essential that the data be collected and presented in an acceptable analytic framework. It is imperative that we do more than that, however. We have to somehow envision what the figures mean in terms of the pattern and quality of daily life for the tens of millions of women we are concerned with. We must get a glimpse into their routines, their customary problems, their familiar burdens and

[2]Michael Harrington, *The Other America* (New York: Macmillan, 1963).

pleasures. We must begin to describe the faces behind these statistics, to fashion new images of the American woman that are in touch with the realities of today. It may take a novelist or at the very least an anthropologist with the sensitivity and compassion of Oscar Lewis to complete that task.[3] But we must at the very least start.

Divorce, Alimony, and the Double Standard of Aging

One additional theoretical problem has to be attended to before we proceed. It will be argued that the lower salaries and reduced opportunities afforded women on the job market do not affect their class standing and status in the society, since women as housewives and daughters enjoy whatever material advantage and prestige is brought to the family by the male breadwinner. Members of the family supposedly share the same rank and are treated as social equals.

The first flaw in this argument has already been exposed. A considerable portion of working women are the main supporters not just of themselves, but of their families. In March 1974, for example, 5.6 million families in the United States were headed by women. That is, 6.8 million women—widowed, divorced, separated, or single—were responsible for raising children in a fatherless family or for supporting parents or other family members.[4] Marriages, it would seem, are less and less "made in heaven" and for life. One out of every three or four marriages today is dissolved; the rate of divorce has been on the increase in the last decades and is still going up. Since women tend to outlive men as well, a good number of them will have to face life as widows even before old age. All of this means that a woman realistically has to figure on entering and staying on the job market in her mature years, no matter how safely ensconced and busily occupied she may presently be as a housewife. The record shows, in fact, that the median age of women in the labor force in 1969 was 39.5[5] Also, of

[3]See, for example, Oscar Lewis, *The Children of Sanchez* (New York: Random House, 1961).

[4]U.S. Department of Labor, Bureau of Labor Statistics, *Monthly Labor Review*, March 1974.

[5]Robert L. Stein, "Women at Work," *Monthly Labor Review*, June 1970, p. 17.

the 72 million women aged sixteen and over in the population, more than half (37 million) had worked at one time or another during the previous year.[6]

Does a divorcee, an abandoned woman, or even a widow continue to enjoy the economic standing and prestige of her former or late mate? Observations suggest not—not at all. With the possible exception of the rare individuals lucky enough to have been born to or to have married great wealth and high status, women left alone in the world have to make it on their own, not just economically, but socially as well. As countless books and articles on the problems of divorcees reveal, very seldom is there a retinue of friends standing by, only rarely does a newly single woman get invitations to social gatherings, and hardly ever are there acceptable and socially promising organizations for her to join. A woman on the loose in her mature years is a social handicap, a potential threat, and a dreaded embarrassment to the couples she used to see socially with her former mate. For most women there is no escape from the lonely world of the formerly married other than joining in the often-frantic activities of a singles club. For *her* there are no fraternal lodges, no sports clubs, no respectable bars—and no hostesses who will welcome her as a valuable addition to the social group. Unless she has unusually high social standing and income, the widow or divorcee will be left to her own resources socially as well as economically. She will even find it harder to get credit in stores or to find acceptance as a buyer of a home or a car. Final recognition was given this widespread problem in an amendment to the Consumer Credit Protection Act (15 U.S. Code 1601) that went into effect November 1975. It is now unlawful for any creditor to discriminate against any credit application on the basis of sex or marital status—but it is to be noted that one may have to file suit to compel enforcement!

To escape from the problems and loneliness of divorced life into another marriage seems to be the most natural course of action. But here a mature woman will find another and more painful barrier to mount: the double standard of aging. Quite simply, as Inge Powell Bell demonstrates in her compelling study, the inevitable physical symptoms of aging make women sexually unattractive

[6]Stein, p. 14.

much earlier than men. For a man "sexual value is defined much more in terms of personality, intelligence and earning power rather than physical appearance. Women, however, must rest their case largely on their bodies."[7]

The consequences are all too well known for women who re-acquaint themselves with the single social life in their forties. Coupled with the decline in status and economic well-being, they have to live with the growing indifference of men toward their looks, toward their sexuality. Men their own ages and even men several years older will be looking for younger women. That option—to seek a much younger partner—is ruled out for most women; our culture has reserved some particularly choice and nasty terms for women who dare go against this norm. And so women in their sexually prime period—from mid-thirties into the fifties—find themselves "put on the shelf" by age definitions that are different for the two sexes.

This is, as Inge Powell Bell shows, most dramatically institutionalized in the cultural rules governing the ages at which one can marry. Men can marry women 15 to 20 years younger than they are, but to go in the other direction—unthinkable! Marriage statistics tell the story very plainly: the age differential is relatively small at the time of the first marriage; but when widowers remarry, the groom is on the average 8.3 years older than his bride; and when divorced men remarry, the gap is 4.5 years. Statistics also prove that women have a harder time remarrying than men. In one study, three-quarters of divorced men were found to have remarried, while only two-thirds of women did. The discrepancy was larger among widows and widowers; among those on their own from five to fourteen years, two-thirds of the men had remarried, but only one-third of the women had.[8]

This cannot be overemphasized: a woman left alone to head her family is usually in a severe economic plight. The median income for the nearly 7 million women who fall into this group was $4,729 in 1973, just slightly above the poverty threshold set by the Social Security Administration for a nonfarm family of four ($4,540). By

[7]Inge Powell Bell, "The Double Standard of Aging," *Trans-Action*, November-December 1970, p. 76.
[8]Bell, p. 78.

comparison, the median income for male-headed families in the same year was $11,600.

The picture emerging from these figures is clearly *not* one of widows and divorcees living high on pensions, alimonies, or child-support payments. In 1974, 54 percent of women family heads were, in fact, in the labor force. Nearly one-third of these earned incomes below the poverty level in 1973. In addition, a study from 1970 shows that less than 30 percent of the meager income enjoyed by all women family heads comes from the late husband, the ex-husband, the father, or any other source.[9]

The implications of these findings are profound, indeed. An American woman today has to face up to the very real possibility that she will live part or most of her adult life alone. Her chances in that regard are one out of every three or four. If she is a widow, the chances of her having to take up work is roughly one out of three, and if she is divorced, two out of three. She is more than likely to have children to support in her new-found single state: in 1974, 59 percent of the children in these one-parent families (white) had working mothers.[10] At the same time, she will have to face the ugly fact that without a husband on the scene, she and her children are more than likely to live close to the poverty level. This, even though she may work full time in addition to the many hours spent daily on housekeeping and child care.

The most disturbing myth still prevailing about American women may be that of the easy, comfortable life obtained for women through divorce settlements. Alimony, it turns out, is awarded only in a miniscule number of cases. In a nationwide study, the judges surveyed revealed that alimony awards were part of the final judgment in only *2 percent* of the cases. Temporary alimony was awarded in 10 percent of the cases in order to allow the wife an opportunity to find a job.[11] The division of property and family assets hardly relieves the situation of the woman who now has to enter the job market with little training and experience in anything but household tasks. A recent review of the cases sug-

[9]Stein, "Women at Work," p. 17.

[10]In black families, the proportion was 45 percent. Elizabeth Waldman, "Children of Working Mothers," *Monthly Labor Review,* January 1975, p. 64.

[11]Quenstedt and Winkler, *ABA Support Committee of the Family Law Section.* (Monograph No. 1 (1965). Quoted in *Drake Law Review,* No. 2 (1975): 285.

gests that in middle- and lower-income groups, the husband's welfare and prospects for remarriage are accorded substantially more weight by judges than the wife's and children's welfare.[12]

Even more explosive of the "gay divorcee" myth are the data pertaining to child support and its collection. A crucial contribution in most cases, this can indeed determine whether a broken family falls above the poverty level or must rely on public assistance. And here are the findings: payments awarded are usually not enough to furnish even *one-half* the actual cost of rearing a child.[13]

But it gets worse. Collection of child support is a hit-and-miss proposition for many broken families in spite of the meager awards ordered by the courts. Another study reveals that within one year after the divorce decree, only 38 percent of the fathers were in full compliance with the support order; 42 percent of the fathers made no payments at all! And by the tenth year, only 13 percent of the fathers were fully complying, and 79 percent were in total noncompliance.[14] The earlier findings of William J. Goode are here confirmed; the situation has, if anything, worsened since he wrote *After Divorce* in the fifties. The courts, as he pointed out, are usually reluctant to jail ex-husbands for nonpayment of child support.[15]

These are not happy prospects. They are, it should be clear, alarming enough for every American woman to take notice of and seek to change the fate that might easily be hers in the years ahead. It is worth focusing, again, on some essential and surprising data. Among all families in the United States in the mid-seventies about one out of eight is headed by a woman. Of all women at work, one out of ten is a family head. Among all poor families, more than two out of five are headed by women. In a study from 1973, it is shown that children in female-headed families are much more likely to be at the low-income level than those in male-headed families—52 percent compared to 8 percent![16]

---

[12]Citizens Advisory Council on the Status of Women, *The Equal Rights Amendment and Alimony and Child Support Laws* 2 (1972) (Washington, D.C.: Government Printing Office, 1972).

[13]Quenstedt and Winkler, *ABA Support Committee,* note 206.

[14]S. Nagel and L. Wetzman, "Woman as Litigants," *Hastings Law Journal* 23 (1971): 171, 189.

[15]William J. Goode, *After Divorce* (Glencoe, Ill.: Free Press, 1956), pp. 220-23.

[16]"Characteristics of the Low Income Population, 1973," *Current Population Survey,* Series P-60, No. 98 (Washington, D.C.: Government Printing Office, 1974).

What is particularly startling about these figures is that they pertain to two classes of people that supposedly command great sympathy among Americans—women trying to raise families on their own and children growing up in fatherless homes.

We are still not through exploring the economic risks facing American women who live without husbands. In 1974 there were nearly 14 million of these women in the labor force. In addition, however, we find several million lone women subsisting on welfare, Social Security, or old-age pensions. It is widely known that most welfare recipients are women who receive their aid through the program called Aid to Families with Dependent Children. In the mid-seventies, we find that more than eight out of every ten welfare recipients are women in the major cities.

Aged women living alone constitute another group of individuals supposedly deserving sympathy and help in our society. In reality, however, they frequently suffer a very bitter fate. The lonely aged poor, of which a strong majority are women, are the single most impoverished group in their subculture of poverty, as Michael Harrington points out.[17] Our aged poor numbered more than 3.4 million persons in 1973, and about three-fourths of aged unrelated individuals were women living without marriage partners or other family members—living alone.[18]

The findings cited above make it overwhelmingly clear that woman's fate in our society today is no longer tied to that of her man to the point where the two may be treated as an entity in terms of economics and status. Women who are self-supporting and women who are heads of families add up to such an impressive number that they must be viewed as separate and major groups within the population. At the same time, indications are strong that as separate groups they are to be found at the bottom ranks of the stratification system. The situation is all the more serious because of the fact that this is a fate that *may* in this day and age befall almost any woman at some point in her life. Abandonment, divorce, and widowhood are not rare and infrequent, but rather quite common experiences for the supposedly fairer and weaker of the sexes. And on her own, without the protection of a mate, the American woman has to face risks and accept situations that are

[17]Michael Harrington, *The Other America* (New York: Macmillan, 1963).
[18]*Current Population Survey*, p. 8.

evidently harder, much harder, to bear than we have previously thought.

It is very questionable, too, whether it is either morally proper or politically defensible to ignore the seemingly great inequities in jobs and education affecting married women on the grounds that they do, after all, belong in the social strata of their husbands. Not only the instability of marriage today, but also the very real need for the wife's income in many families, argues against treating the woman as a mere appendage, socially and economically speaking.

In the early seventies 41 percent of all married women were in the labor force, and in no less than 6.4 million of these families the husband's yearly income (1973) was below $7,000. The data also show that in more than a quarter of the two-income families, the wife contributes 40 percent or more of the total income. Wives work, more often than not, because they have to—to maintain what is only a barely adequate standard of living in the contemporary United States.

Are Women Not "Good Enough"?

What do we find, then, when we focus on the American woman's share of earnings and opportunities on the job market? Is she, as our data so far seem to suggest, still incontestably on the bottom? And is it the stratification system that determines her chances to enjoy what the American man has come to expect once he enters the labor market?

Even in the mid-seventies—with several years of disclosures about sex discrimination behind us and new legislation in effect to end it on the job market—we find the general disparity in income between the sexes to be nothing less than dramatic. Sex bias, concluded the President's Task Force on Women's Rights and Responsibilities in 1970, takes a greater economic toll than race bias. This conclusion is further confirmed in data from the Bureau of Labor Statistics in 1974; as Table 2.1 shows, this trend has been aggravated.

American women in 1974 earned about 60 percent of the wages enjoyed by men. That, in fact, points to a deterioration of women's earning capacities in the last two decades: in 1955 American

TABLE 2.1   Median Weekly Earnings of Wage
and Salary Workers by Selected Characteristics

	1967	1974	Percent Change
White men	$130	$209	60.8
Black men	90	160	77.8
White women	79	125	58.2
Black women	63	117	85.7

Source: Bureau of Labor Statistics data in Bradshaw and Stinson, "Trends in Weekly Earnings," *Monthly Labor Review,* August 1975.

women on the average took home 63.9 percent of the wages earned by men.

The main reason for this conspicuous gap is often said to be the *types* of jobs held by women. In 1973, 13.1 million women were employed in either the service or trade industries. Typical occupations were sales or clerical personnel, restaurant workers, and domestic servants—and all of these are relatively low-paying jobs. Men, on the other hand, find employment as professional and technical workers, managers, proprietors, craftsmen, foremen, factory workers—all jobs that pay better. And 70 percent of men working are employed in these categories.[19]

Although this fact explains the earning gap between men and women to some degree, it does not, by any means, excuse it. What has to be explored is *why* women end up in the lower-paying jobs. In order for us to accept their fate as just and proper in a democratic society, we would have to be shown that women either do not have the capabilities for any other work and/or have no desire for it.

That the first proposition is patent nonsense is in the first place shown by the fact that some women, a significant number in terms of demonstrable ability, have made it into almost every job category dominated by and presumed to be better suited to men. In the

[19]"Rebelling Women—The Reason," *U.S. News and World Report,* April 13, 1970, p. 35.

United States, these "loophole" women, as Caroline Bird calls them,[20] may be so few in some trades and professions that they could be said to be only exceptions to the rule. But in other modern societies women have moved in *large* numbers into the same fields. In Israel, in the Scandinavian countries, and in the Soviet Union, for example, women have proven themselves as doctors, dentists, engineers, architects, scientists, and skilled technicians and operators for many years. Their most spectacular advances have come in the Soviet Union, where they now constitute 75 percent of the doctors, 83 percent of the dentists, 28 percent of the engineers, and 38 percent of the scientists. The respective percentages for the United States in 1970 were 6.5, 2.1, 1.2, and 7.[21]

Surely no one is going to argue that the American woman is less talented and capable than the Soviet woman! Given the number of suits filed by women denied access to certain jobs in the last few years, it is going to be equally difficult to defend the theory that American women are not interested in the higher-paid professions. To suggest that they are not is, after all, an insult to their good practical sense.

It is worth noting, too, that in one of the most important professions from which women have been virtually excluded, the evidence indicates that they could contribute a great deal indeed. According to the U.S. Department of Labor, two-thirds as many women as men (8 and 12 percent of the population, respectively) have engineering aptitude.[22]

The grave error and disastrous effect of the concept of "masculine" and "feminine" occupations is seen most clearly in the skilled trades and crafts, as Janice Neipert Hedges points out. These are jobs that bring with them high earnings, but where training costs are low. Women make up only 3 percent of the craftsmen and less than 1 percent of the skilled tradesmen of this country. These are simply not "women's jobs"—the prejudice against women here is as deep as it is rampant. And yet "the basic requirements that run through the skilled trades are finger and hand dexterity and eye-hand coordination"—abilities required for typ-

[20]Caroline Bird, *Born Female* (New York: Pocket Books, 1969).
[21]Cynthia Fuchs Epstein, *Woman's Place* (Berkeley: University of California Press, 1970, p. 12.
[22]Stein, "Women at Work," p. 26.

ing and many other clerical occupations performed by women—"together with aptitude for form and space perception." The particular combination of aptitudes required for a number of crafts are found as frequently among female as male students in the eleventh grade. Nor can strength requirements be considered a real obstacle to women's access to these relatively profitable fields, since most require only light strength. Also, Miss Hedges reminds us, some women are stronger than some men.[23]

We have to conclude, then, that women are in the lower-paid occupations for the simple reason that these are jobs considered "fitting" for women—this is the only rank to which they are welcomed. Moreover, the prejudice in operation here, shared by men and women alike, is not a "natural" one. The fact that it has been wholly or significantly overcome in other societies is sufficient proof of that. It is, one must suspect, due to a bias built into the institutional structure of our society, particularly that part of the structure endowed with legitimate authority to distribute goods and resources among us.

This is a point we shall return to and dwell on at considerable length. What is suggested here is another way of hypothesizing that the stratification system operates to the definite and disastrous disadvantage of women who have to make it on their own.

One specific example offers an important illustration of this general proposition. Education could and should make for significant differences in the status and earnings of different groups in an "achieving society." Can women's lack of advances on the job market perhaps be attributed to their inadequacies in this regard? Are they simply not prepared—as far as formal education is concerned—to take up competition with men?

Startlingly, the record shows just the opposite. The Department of Labor tells us that women eighteen years of age and over in the labor force have slightly more schooling than do the general population.[26] The median years of school completed by women workers is higher than that of men workers.[24]

The full extent of the handicap suffered by educated women is revealed by the following fact: as shown by the underlined entries in Table 2.2, in 1973 a woman college graduate could expect to

---

[23]Stein, p. 26.
[24]U.S. Department of Labor, Women's Bureau, *The Earnings Gap* (March 1974).

TABLE 2.2   Median Income of Year-round Full-time Workers,
by Sex and Years of School Completed, 1973
(Persons 25 years of age and over)

Years of school completed	Median income		Women's median income as percentage of men's
	Women	Men	
Elementary school:			
Less than 8 years	$ 4,369	$ 7,521	58.1
8 years	5,135	9,406	54.6
High school:			
1 to 3 years	5,513	10,401	53.0
4 years	6,623	12,017	55.1
College:			
1 to 3 years	7,593	13,090	58.0
4 years	9,057	15,503	58.4
5 years or more	11,340	17,726	64.0

Source: U.S. Department of Labor, Women's Bureau, *The Earnings Gap* (March 1974).

earn $349 less per year than a male who had only graduated from elementary school!

Sex Bias Gone Rampant

Sex bias still seems to operate throughout the job market. The real measure of its effect can best be obtained through a comparison of income and opportunities afforded men and women in the job categories occupied by both. "Equal pay for equal work" is, after all, a time-honored and thoroughly American principle, now presumed to be enforced by the Equal Pay Act (1963) and Executive Order 11246 issued in December 1973. To suggest that women still do not obtain their due on the job market in terms of either wages or opportunities is to fire a very serious charge, indeed, at the nature of our socioeconomic structure. Is it as inherently sexist as the data so far seem to suggest?

As indicated by Table 2.3, which compares median wages for women and men in the same broad job categories, women are at a

TABLE 2.3   Median Wage or Salary Income of Year-round
Full-time Workers, by Sex and Nonfarm
Occupational Group, 1973
(Persons 14 years of age and over)

Major occupational group	*Median wage or salary income*		*Women's median wage or salary income as percentage of men's*
	Women	*Men*	
Professional, technical workers	$9,095	$13,945	65.2
Managers, administrators (except farm)	7,998	14,737	54.3
Sales workers	4,674	12,031	38.8
Clerical workers	6,458	10,619	60.8
Craft and kindred workers	6,315	11,308	55.8
Operatives (including transport)	5,420	9,481	57.2
Service workers (except private household)	4,745	8,112	58.5
Private household workers	2,243	a	—
Nonfarm laborers	5,286	8,037	65.8

Source: U.S. Department of Labor, *The Earnings Gap.*

a Fewer than 75,000 men.

serious disadvantage relative to men even when they are found in
the same occupation groups. The higher-paid jobs within each are
clearly not for women. Here, the retail trades offer a striking example of the sex discrimination which is still in effect. In 1973
about 2.3 million women were year-round full-time sales clerks.
Their median salary that year was $4,674—exactly 38.8 percent of
the median earnings of men engaged in the same type of work.
How does such a sharp disparity come about and escape legal
challenges?[25] The answer is primarily that men and women were
assigned to sell different things. Where salaries, in 1971, exceeded
$110 weekly (e.g., car sales, building materials, and farm equip-
ment), we find only 4.1 percent of the female sales personnel as
compared to 18 percent of the male sales personnel. Women are

[25]U.S. Department of Labor, Bureau of Labor Statistics, *U.S. Working Women: A
Chartbook* (1975).

clustered in the lower-paying trades: nearly 36 percent of the saleswomen were in ready-to-wear sales or eating and drinking places, with salaries under $70 weekly. Only about 15 percent of the men were employed in these types of sales.[26]

Channeling of women into the lower-status, lower-paying positions is a major reason for the disparities which are demonstrated here. But it is also well known that women frequently are paid less than men for doing identical work. The discrimination in effect here, clearly illegal, can be disguised by giving men different job titles; a "charwoman" becomes a "janitor" or a "caretaker," for example.[27] Yet it is more than anything else the low degree of social mobility afforded women that keeps them on the bottom of the social ladder.

Two professions dominated by women offer the most striking illustration of this principle. The domination is in terms of numbers only—in status, salaries, and power, the relatively few men in these occupations outrank their female colleagues persistently and dramatically. They do so because it is *they* who are offered the opportunities, *they* who are awarded the honors, and *they* who are given the responsibilities that carry with them influence and authority. *Formally*, however, salary differentials based on sex in these professions have been abolished.

In the case of *teaching*, for example, where 1.4 million women found employment in 1969, 85 percent of the women were found in elementary school, in the lower grades. Status and pay is slightly lower there than it is in high school, where women composed only 46 percent of the teaching staff. The drop in the percentage of women teaching in secondary schools has been sharp; they constituted 57 percent of high school teachers in 1957. But the decline of women elementary school principals has been really dramatic. John Hoyle offers a very revealing glimpse into the nature of the problem in an article titled "Who Shall Be Principal—A Man or a Woman?" In 1928, 55 percent of elementary school principals were women; in 1948, 41 percent; in 1958, 38 percent; and in 1968, the

---

[26]U.S. Department of Labor, *Employment and Earning Statistics for the U.S., 1909–1971* (1973).

[27]Joy Osofsky and Harold Feldman, *Fact Sheet on Women* (Ithaca, N.Y.: Cornell University Press, 1969).

figure was reported to have dropped to 22 percent.[28] This means that men, who constituted only 12 percent of the teaching force in elementary schools, held 78 percent of the elementary principalships!

How did this happen? Obviously, superintendents and boards of education think that men are more capable administrators. The boards, incidentally, are heavily male-dominated and the superintendents of large school districts almost exclusively male.[29] Do their choices reflect a reasoned and informed judgment as to who makes the best principal? Or is this yet another case of sex bias gone rampant?

Reviewing recent research findings as to what qualities and characteristics are required for principals to be effective, Hoyle suggests that there are no reasons for preferring men. In fact, women rate better than men as "democratic leaders" and in administrative skills. It was not true, moreover, that teachers prefer male principals. They rated them about equally. One authoritative study by Kenneth McIntyre concluded that "research does not show men to be superior to women in the principalship—in fact, the little evidence we have suggests the opposite conclusion."[30]

To clinch the argument, it should be pointed out that the record shows men who were appointed principals had less teaching experience than their female colleagues who came to be so honored. Of the males, 66.7 percent had *less* than six years of teaching experience at the time of their advancement. Conversely, 88 percent of the female principals had *more* than six years of teaching experience when they started their jobs.

Sex discrimination in education is, of course, of tremendous importance for the opportunities and advances of women into any field, and we shall discuss it fully at some later point. What has been shown so far is that in the profession that women have moved into in the greatest number, the social mobility offered them is severely limited. The powers that be in education, heavily male in composi-

[28]John Hoyle, "Who Shall Be Principal—A Man or a Woman?" *National Elementary Principal,* no. 3 (January 1969); 23-25.

[29]In Minnesota, for example, it was found that there were *no* female superintendents of schools.

[30]Kenneth E. McIntyre, "The Selection of Elementary School Principals," quoted in Hoyle, "Who Shall Be Principal?"

tion at all levels, give pronounced preferential treatment to men. Women, again, have to take the back seat.

Library work is another profession dominated by women. In 1968, 95,000 women were employed in this category, making up about 90 percent of all librarians. What does the status of the sexual majority in this profession reveal about the social mobility of women?

The first fact to stare us in the face is this: here, too, women have suffered a decline in status that is quite drastic. In an article entitled "The Widening Sex Gap," Anita R. Schiller points out that in 1930 women had nineteen and men fifty-five of the chief librarianships in seventy-four large colleges and universities. A check of the same positions in these libraries today reveals that only four of them are held by women and seventy by men. Among academic librarians, specifically, there are nearly twice as many women as men. Yet not one of the largest academic libraries in the United States is headed by a woman.[31]

Salary differentials for men and women in this profession are also striking. For one thing, the median yearly salary for men is $8,990 and for women $7,455—about $1,500 less. In spite of the far greater numbers of women librarians, we find that the proportion of men in higher positions is much higher than that of women. The chance for a woman to become a head librarian is only about half as good as the chance of a man. The libraries women get to administer are also generally smaller and the salaries lower. Thus among chief librarians, the median yearly salary for men is $11,700, while for women it is only $8,300. Men who are *not* chief librarians tend to do as well as or better than women who *are*. The gap cannot be ascribed to differences in educational level or experience between the sexes. Anita R. Schiller points out that women with the *same* amount of professional experience and education as men are compensated at a *lower* rate. The more experience they acquire, the greater their disadvantage. The data available show very clearly that in this profession, too, "women are the underprivileged majority." Although they are freely accepted into its ranks, their future advancement in the profession is limited.

[31]Anita R. Schiller, "The Widening Sex Gap," *Library Journal*, March 15, 1969, pp. 1097–1101.

We have, then, proof of yet another case of restricted social mobility for women. Others can be brought up, so many others that the exploration could easily become tedious. The professions we have concerned ourselves with here are of central importance because they are among the very few that women have made inroads into and even come to dominate in numbers. Also, because salaries and ranks and advancements in these professions are supposedly determined by educational attainment, experience, and demonstrated ability, and no other considerations, the bias introduced is illegitimate, if not illegal. When we find it operating as we have to the serious detriment of hundreds of thousands of women professionals, we can only draw the conclusion that if there is a sex gap in *these* fields of endeavor, it is a reflection of a bias that is as pervasive as it is deeply embedded in American institutions. In income and in social mobility, working women have been shown to be so severely disadvantaged that one suspects forces in operation that are as yet beyond the grasp and influence of most of us.

three

Institutional Sexism

"Sex prejudice," in the words of poet Eve Merriam, "is the only prejudice now considered socially acceptable."[1]

To that, any number of women seeking equal opportunities in higher education and on the job market are likely to say "Amen!" What is remarkable about the sex bias operative in these fields is not just that it is so widespread, but that it still can be frankly expressed. Story after story is passed around among women telling of the semicomic and yet revolting prejudices expressed by male bosses, colleagues, and professors. For that matter, women themselves can be quite expert at denigrating their own sex. Although an educated, progressive man—or woman—would think twice, to say the least, before talking about someone of a different race being unfit for certain jobs, having less of a potential for development, and also having less of a "need" for advancement and higher income, that same person will not hesitate to say *exactly* that and *more* of a woman.

Typical of the comments by male employers are the following: "Your qualifications for this job seem just fine, but we just don't hire women in this category." It can be put more bluntly, of course: "This field is not for women." "Women don't fit in here." "You may be an exception, but women are generally too emotional and unre-

---

[1] Quoted in Cynthia Fuchs Epstein, *Women's Place* (Berkeley: University of California Press, 1970), p. 34.

liable under stress to handle this kind of job." "Can you type instead?"

Even former President Nixon's Labor Secretary James D. Hodgson publicly recognized the profound sex bias in the labor market. Job discrimination against women, declared Hodgson in the summer of 1970, is "more subtle and more pervasive than against any other minority group."[2]

This sobering conclusion is given support by prominent black women. Many report, as did Congresswoman Shirley Chisholm and lawyer Pauli Murray, that in their lives they have experienced far more discrimination on the grounds of sex than of race.[3] A frank management consultant, quoted by Caroline Bird, typifies this common attitude: in response to a job query by a woman executive, he confessed, "I'm not ready for a woman. But, boy, would I love to get hold of a good Negro!"[4]

The parallels in attitudes toward women and blacks in America have been noted by expert observers like Gunnar Myrdal and Helen Hacker. Both groups are held to be "childlike," inferior in intelligence, emotional, and incapable of genius. Both are said to be "all right in their places" and to really prefer staying there. They—women and blacks—are also recognized as being typically capable of deviousness, intrigue, and intuitive powers. Those of both groups who accept their role in life without complaint are the "good" blacks or the "real" women, and those who want change are "uppity" or "sick." The stock response to those who complain about their role is: "What do you want—to be white?" or "What do you want—to be a man?"

Shirley Chisholm has given testimony to the persistence of these attitudes:

> To keep them in their place, the same characteristics are imputed to women as to blacks—that they are more childish, emotional and irresponsible than men, that they are of lower intelligence than men, that they need protection, that they are happiest in routine, undemanding jobs, and that they lack ambition and executive ability.[5]

---

[2] Quoted in the *San Francisco Chronicle Magazine,* July 26, 1970, p. 7.

[3] Alice S. Rossi, "Job Discrimination and What Women Can Do about It," *Atlantic Monthly,* March 1970, pp. 99–103.

[4] Caroline Bird, *Born Female* (New York: Pocket Books, 1969), p. 125.

[5] Testimony before a House subcommittee considering legislation opposing discrimination against women. Quoted in *The Militant,* July 17, 1970, p. 18.

Of late, one difference has been introduced. The civil rights movement has succeeded in removing all *legal* barriers to full equality for blacks; it has also captured the attention and sympathy of the media and, most importantly, shown itself to be a formidable political force. Racial prejudice, as a consequence, has become a political liability—and a social embarrassment. It is not quite so with sexual prejudice!

The greater distance women have to travel is evidenced most clearly in attitudes and responses to *their* liberation movement. Civil rights groups are now accorded respect, however grudgingly; both their goals and their methods are treated seriously and the former accepted as thoroughly legitimate by most Americans. The claims of women, however, no matter how convincingly demonstrated, are still viewed as irrelevant or peripheral matters by most, and "Women's Lib"—even in the mid-seventies—remains the butt of many a male joke.

The insistence on using the term *girls* when speaking to or about adult females illustrates this point very well. The time has long since passed that anyone dared call a black male "boy." Both terms are equally insulting when applied to mature adults; yet the designation of women to the ranks of the childlike is still widespread, and reminders from feminists on this point are responded to with profound irritation and/or mirth by many a male. Though women in the movement have learned much from the civil rights struggle, they have not quite succeeded in changing the common images of members of their own sex—as essentially frivolous, indulged specimens.

"You can't make that demand. We haven't even conceded it to blacks yet!" was the response of a council member of the American Psychological Association to a request by women professionals in 1969 that accreditation be withheld from departments that cannot show nondiscrimination. The point made was quickly noted by one shocked female psychologist: "This just shows that women are even a second-class minority group. We can only ask for what blacks have already got."[6]

---

[6]Quoted in Jo Freeman, "The Revolution Is Happening in Our Minds," *College and University Business,* February 1970, p. 67.

The Racist Analogy

What all of this points to is that women are suffering from a phenomenon closely akin to *racism*. That term has come to mean a system of social, political, and psychological pressures that tends to suppress a group with certain biologically determined characteristics. To prove the existence of racism, it must be shown that the suppression goes beyond or is contrary to normal divisions of class. A black unskilled laborer may be suppressed and exploited, but it is a case of racist oppression only if his vulnerability and suffering are greater than those of his white co-worker. As a black, he must be shown to have been made a member of a class within a class. A victim of racism will thus be systematically relegated to a sub-stratum within the major stratum he or she belongs to by occupation and educational achievement.

This seems to be precisely the system in operation in regard to women on the labor market. If anything, the supression of women is even more systematic and severe, although a great deal more subtle, than that of black men. At the same time, it must be recognized that there *are* avenues of escape open to women that are pretty much foreclosed to other minority members.[7] Marriage still is foremost among these, although its value as an "escape," as noted, has been severely diminished with the greatly increased impermanency of the institution.

It must also be recognized that in the female group, it is *black* women who suffer the most. They have to carry on their backs the double burden of being black and being female in a society where both identities carry with them distinct and serious disadvantages. How staggering that burden can be is indicated by the fact that among all major groups in our society, poverty is *most* likely to hit a nonwhite family headed by a woman: 51.4 percent of such families were on or below the poverty line in 1973. The highest rates of unemployment today are also among black female youths (23.3 percent for high school graduates).[8]

----

[7] We use the term *minority* here as a sociological and not a statistical concept, the identifying factor being the presence of discrimination against group members.

[8] U.S. Department of Labor, Employment Standards Administration, *Facts on Women Workers of Minority Races* (1974).

But in the larger society black and white women share the common burden of discrimination based upon sex. In reviewing the most recent data of incomes for men and women, it was shown that the gap between black and white women is closing—in 1974 white women earned $8 more weekly than black women on the average (see Table 2.1). The gap in earnings between men and women remains *large* and has, in fact, increased in recent years. It must also be remembered that it is women, black and white, who are asked to carry the double burden of raising children and caring for the home while working outside the home. With increasing and alarming frequency they also have to do this without any aid of a man.

"Woman as Nigger" is, indeed, the provocative title of an article by Gayle Rubin. In it, she points out that "people are more sophisticated about blacks than they are about women: black history courses do not have to begin by convincing people that blacks are not in fact genetically better suited to dancing than to learning."[9] That women are capable of different roles is still not recognized. Notably, the word *sex* was included in the 1964 Civil Rights Act as a joke. Miss Rubin reminds us that it was opposed by all liberals on the ground that it would make the whole Civil Rights Act more difficult to pass!

The racism we are discussing here, most aptly referred to as *sexism*, is not just a phenomenon in the minds of men and women in America. To the extent that it exists, it is, as are all systems that maintain relationships of dominance and subordination, *institutionalized*. It also has an *ideology*, implanted and perpetrated by institutions centrally located in the political socialization process. Last but not least, it has an *interest structure* that provides the underlying rationale and dynamic for the ongoing process.

ERA and Its Enemies

Controls and discriminatory patterns affecting any group are always maintained through legal codes and/or institutionalized behavior so well entrenched that the persons involved often are not conscious of operating in a racist manner. In a democracy, one sooner or later has to conform with the basic principle of equality

[9]Gayle Rubin, "Woman as Nigger," *The Argus*, March 28–April 11, 1970, p. 7.

under the law, and it is thus mainly the institutional web that upholds racist patterns of behavior. Strikingly, in comparing the status and rights of women and black men in our society, we find—again—that it is women who have had to take the back seats when it comes to the elimination of legal codes sanctifying discrimination.

There is, in the first place, the obvious and glaring omission of women from the Fourteenth and Fifteenth Amendments. Sex was left out of both: voting rights and equality of rights under the law were guaranteed to all citizens without regard to race, creed, or color—as long as they were male. It took more than half a century of bitter struggle to win for women the first and most basic right in a democracy, the vote—accorded minority males in 1867. The basic rights guaranteed to men in our society by the Fifteenth Amendment were yet to be extended to women more than a hundred years after its passage. As late as 1975 only thirty-four states had passed the Equal Rights Amendment—four less than the required thirty-eight for its ratification. All the amendment proposes is that "equality of rights under the law shall not be denied or abridged by the United States or by any state on account of sex." Elementary enough, it would seem.

The forces and arguments arrayed against the Equal Rights Amendment (ERA) are quite revealing, both in terms of the attitudes and the dynamics of sexism in this society. Opposition to the amendment on Capitol Hill was led by Congressman Emanuel Celler (D., N.Y.) and by Senator Sam Ervin (D., N.C.). According to Celler, "There is more difference between a man and a woman than between a horse chestnut and a chestnut horse."[10] His tactic in dealing with what he called "the blunderbuss amendment" was to refuse hearings or reports on it out of the House Judiciary Committee which he chaired. It took a discharge petition, a highly unusual and risky procedure in Congress, to get the amendment out on the floor. Representative Martha Griffiths (D., Mich.) led the fight to get the amendment out of committee and to ensure its passage in the House. The final vote, on August 10, 1970, was an overwhelming 352 in favor, 15 opposed.

[10]Quoted in Diane Schulder, "Women and the Law," *Atlantic Monthly*, March 1970, pp. 103–5.

In the Senate the venerable Sam Ervin waxed lyrical and biblical as he led the opposition, first in the Judiciary Committee and then on the floor. If the amendment were ratified, he proclaimed, it would mean women had to be drafted and "sent into battle to have their fair forms blasted into fragments by the bombs and the shells of the enemy."[11] Amendment after amendment were offered by him: to exempt women from the draft, from combat service, to ensure sexual privacy, to retain protective laws in effect for the "gentle sex." One by one these arguments were countered by sup-porters, and the Senate finally passed the ERA without change on March 22, 1972, with an 84–8 vote.

It had been a hard and long fight for the women's groups and the congresswomen who worked for the passage. It turned out, however, that this was just the beginning. Major opposition soon emerged at the state level, where approval now had to be won by at least thirty-eight states. It was a motley crew of enemies at first: the AFL-CIO, John Birch Society, National States' Rights party, White Citizens Council, Young Americans for Freedom, Ku Klux Klan, Christian Crusade, Communist party, and Socialist Workers party. For the union movement, opposition to the amendment was dropped in October 1973 because of pressure by union women and the increasingly clear fact that the fear of elimination of protective laws for women was largely unfounded; these were to be extended to men. The forces remaining in opposition were now overwhelm-ingly of the conservative right. "Stop ERA," a well-financed nationwide organization created just to fight the amendment, had as its head Phyllis Schafley, self-proclaimed housewife but long-time activist in politics and author of several right-wing tracts. Her arguments in legislative tracts and before the media invariably stressed the grave dangers inherent in the ERA to woman's *only proper* and noble role, that of adored wife and mother. In total disregard of the realities staring them in the face, she and her followers would charge that the precious protected position of the wife, her right not to work, and family cohesion itself were about to be destroyed. Prostitution, too, was bound to flourish as women are sent into combat and have to share toilets with men! Ludicrous as these arguments are to anyone familiar with the

[11]*Congressional Quarterly Weekly Report* 20, March 25, 1972, p. 693.

actual data concerning women on the labor market and women heads of households, Stop ERA still made distressingly successful inroads within state legislatures. Both access and clout were provided by the backing and ample financing of right-wing groups and parts of the insurance industry.[12] The greatest opposition to ERA, typically, came from the South. As of 1975, only two of the eleven former Confederate states had ratified the amendment.

Yet the reaction of women across the country, as even this symbolic recognition of their claim to equality was to be denied, gave a number of high-powered politicians pause. The roster of supporters of the ERA in the end included virtually every respected and well-established women's organization. Candidates took heed, often at the urging of their wives; only one of those in the race for the presidential nomination until the end of 1976—Ronald Reagan—held out against all advice and reason.

There is a very real danger, however, in putting too much emphasis on the fight to win passage for the ERA. Just as the Nineteenth Amendment turned out to give nothing to women except the *basis* for political representation and power, so the ERA *cannot* be expected to do the job of eliminating deeply embedded patterns of discrimination on the job market and in politics—not to say social life. Other tools have been available for some years now thanks to the sustained efforts of women's rights advocates in the political arena: the Equal Pay Act, Title IX of the Educational Amendments of 1972, the Women's Education Equity Act of 1973, the Comprehensive Training and Employment Act of 1973, for example. All these do, however, is to *open the way* for legal challenges against sex discrimination in employment and education. The same will be true for the ERA when and if it comes into effect. It could be a cruel disillusionment, indeed, for women who have come to look at its passage as the end-all, the final blow to the oldest and most pervasive system of discrimination in the land.

As we shall see, it is ultimately the common images of women and their proper roles in society that will have to change. Without that, the systematic channeling of women into low-pay, low-status jobs, the subtle but persistent ways to exclude women from the centers of power, will not come to an end.

[12]Lisa C. Wohl, "The Sweetheart of the Silent Majority," *Ms.,* March 1974.

What will have to be fought first of all is the "benign neglect"—or stubborn refusal to face the new social and economic realities confronting American women.

In the early seventies, for instance, working hours for women were still limited by law in thirty-six states. In twenty of these states women were also expressly prohibited from working more than eight hours a day or forty-eight hours a week. They are thus protected from the opportunity of earning any substantial overtime pay—and from promotion to jobs requiring much overtime. Women were also prohibited from entering certain occupations and industries in twenty-six states—usually occupations and industries where the average pay is higher than that in job categories occupied by women. The suffocating paternalism of the law can be explicit, as it is in Michigan, where the code states: "No female shall be given any task disproportionate to her strength, nor shall she be employed in any place detrimental to her morals, her health, and her capacity for motherhood."[13]

This is not to say that there is a deliberate or consciously evolved conspiracy among male bosses and colleagues to prevent the advancement of women into more profitable fields. That such is the *effect* of the numerous objections and reservations raised concerning women's fitness or abilities for certain work is quite clear. But the effectiveness of sexism on the labor market depends on how well sexist differentiation and sexist controls operate in other institutional sectors. If, for instance, men and women alike can be convinced through the socialization process alone that woman's place is in the home and/or that women are less logically inclined and more emotionally unstable than men, then the sanctions of a legal framework may not be needed to maintain patterns of discrimination and control. As the authors of an illuminating work on institutional racism have made clear, discriminatory behavior has become so well institutionalized that individuals generally do not have to exercise a choice to operate in a racist manner. The choices have already been prestructured. The individual has only to conform to the operating norms of the organization he is involved with and the institution will do the discriminating for him.[14]

[13]*Life,* September 4, 1950, p. 18.
[14]Louis Knowles and Kenneth Prewitt, *Institutional Racism in America* (Englewood Cliffs, N.J.: Prentice-Hall, 1969), p. 142.

The techniques for keeping women down are nevertheless overt, far more so than those used to maintain white superiority. Take, for example, the specification for males in the "Help Wanted" columns of publications today, which is illegal under Title VII of the Civil Rights Act of 1964. Any comparison of the jobs offered men with those offered women quickly makes obvious how severe is the opportunity gap between the sexes. Efforts to abolish this particular discrimination have so far proved useless; a challenge of the practice caused it to be abolished for a brief period in 1969, but it was then resumed in nearly all major publications on the grounds that it was the only practical way to advertise jobs. Consider, now, what would surely happen today if employers publicly specified "whites only" in the "Help Wanted" columns! Even in the Civil Service such flagrant violations of fair-employment principles are quite common as far as women are concerned. A survey of the Civil Service Commission some years ago disclosed that 94 percent of the requests received from government agencies for top management jobs specified men.[15]

Just how gross and glaring the put-down of women on the *highest* official levels can be was unwittingly demonstrated by the White House in the fall of 1970. The occasion was a state dinner given by President Nixon for Mexican President Diaz Ordaz in San Diego. The fifty night-shift waitresses on duty at the Hotel del Coronado were plainly told by the hotel management that they wouldn't be needed for this auspicious event. In such grand company, the presence of male waiters was required, compliments of the White House. This one time, however, in a year of women's liberation ferment, the offense was not passed over lightly. Protests were lodged, letters poured in both from the waitresses and from women activists, and the White House hastened to change its plans and simply *add* fifty male waiters, maintaining the fifty female waitresses on duty as usual. Asked then why the word went out to hire only men for the additional help needed, the press secretary in charge explained that it was because "the manner in which you serve usually requires a male waiter trained to serve in this manner." This meant, she added, when further pressed, "serving by

[15]Adrienne Koch, "Two Cheers for Equality," in Seymour M. Farber and Roger H. L. Wilson, eds., *The Potential of Women* (New York: McGraw-Hill, 1963), p. 212.

platter."[16] An operation too complex and difficult for women? Only in the context of institutional sexism can such insensitivity on the part of the presidential office be comprehended. Consider the reaction if the original fifty had been black!

The "Marginality" of Women Workers

The evidence so far indicates that woman's role in the economy today is confined to that of employee and consumer. Women executives or women bosses, as a survey by the *Harvard Business Review* points out, are so few and far between that they might as well be left out of the picture.[17] As for the much-touted wealth of American women, investigation shows it to be of minimal importance for the exertion of influence and control of business operations. We shall come back to this point in a later chapter; for now it is enough to disclose that women constitute only one-third of the top wealth holders of this country, that they come by their money late in life (one-third of them are widows), and that their assets, besides being usually handled by male managers and executives, are by and large of the kind that are not easily converted into cash for financial maneuvers.[18]

Exclusion from ownership and/or control of industry and business has far-reaching consequences for any group in our society. For women, as for black men, it limits their strength and opportunities in many noneconomic areas of life. It is also, as the authors of *Institutional Racism* point out, a major element in defining the constraints of racism.[19] For a woman—as for a black man—this means that we can best comprehend her basic role if we consider her as a seller of labor in the job market. But for a woman, we have to also consider her role as an *unsalaried* worker, uncovered by any laws regulating either hours, benefits, or manner of work. Woman as a housewife is, in this sense, the most underprivileged of all laborers. That she may and often does share in the income and prestige coming to her husband does not change the fact that this

---

[16]*San Francisco Chronicle*, September 2, 1970, p. 5.

[17]Quoted in Epstein, *Woman's Place*, p. 6.

[18]See Roger Lampman, *The Share of Top Wealth Holders in National Wealth, 1956* (Princeton; Princeton University Press, 1962).

[19]Knowles and Prewitt, *Institutional Racism*, p. 146.

award is meted out voluntarily. The housework performed by her is not recognized as sufficiently socially useful to require the governmental protection extended to other types of labor. One might say that a housewife is equally a seller in the job market. For her efforts she gets whatever marriage can offer—with no guarantee of either salary, benefits, or tenure in office.

Our primary focus is still on the woman at work, but it must be understood that the role of the housewife in the economy is inextricably tied to the role of the female employee. The sexual dualism on the labor market is in no small measure due to the acceptance by women of the former role as an—or *the*—essential one. The differently structured set of opportunities offered women are defended on the basis of this ideology, at the same time that the supply of women to the job market can be more easily expanded and constricted because, presumably, women can always return to "home base." New job opportunities for women come only during periods of a tight labor market, when the pool of male labor is drying up. Women then constitute a reserve labor force, to be used if and when male employers, and not the workers themselves, find it opportune.

It is in this, and only in this, sense that women workers are *marginal* to the labor force. Their involvement and activities on the job market are of central importance both to the women themselves and to the employers who engage their services. But a labor boss can afford to be far more high-handed in dismissing women than men. He can also send out calls for women to come in for seasonal work and keep them for just the "right" period to avoid paying for leaves, pensions, and other fringe benefits. And he can, above all, justify the lower pay offered women on the basis that women, after all, are not the family breadwinners. They "just don't need" as much as men.

The major flaw in this proposition has already been exposed: we have seen that the majority of women, at least 25 million in number, work because of stark material, and not fancied or real psychological, need. But the *myth* holds sway and the economic structure continues to provide job earnings and opportunities in a vastly unequal manner for men and women. Sex consequently divides the job market into more distinct and different sectors than does race. A whole array of jobs are designated as women's jobs, and these are almost without exception jobs that offer incomes below the median income of males. How strong and insidious the web of discrimination is can best be illustrated by a look at some of the major occupation groups of employed women over the last four decades. In 1940, women made up 40.1 percent of service workers; in 1974, 55 percent; in 1940 women were 52.6 percent of clerical workers and 27.9 percent of sales workers; in 1974 the percentages of women in the same categories were 78 percent and 42 percent respectively. On the other hand, women's share of positions as technical and professional workers *deteriorated* in the same time span from 45.4 percent in 1940 to 40 percent in 1974.[20] What has happened is that as women have moved into the labor market in greater numbers, they have consistently been channeled into the lower-status occupations and to a great extent kept out of the higher-paid ones. The result is a deterioration of the position of working women in terms of their share of income, status, and social mobility in the last decades.

Sexism in the job market operates, then, basically in two ways: (1) by confining women largely to the positions considered "suitable" for them, that is, the lesser-paid and lower-prestige positions; and (2) by limiting women to specific job classifications and production units within the establishments that hire both men and women. Here, occupational ceilings are set for women in nearly every instance. For them to advance to positions of responsibility and leadership, it is necessary that they be "twice as good as men," as innumerable women have testified. Women are quite simply in a subordinate position and it seems that they are meant to stay there.

Who Benefits?

It stands to reason that someone benefits from this situation. To say that society benefits is a misstatement as glaring as it is shallow. Societies are human constructs that *can* take a variety of forms and *should*, given our value system, take the form that offers the maximum number of people the maximum opportunities for a good

---

[20]U.S. Department of Labor, Bureau of Labor Statistics, *U.S. Working Women: A Chartbook* (1975), chart 10.

life. Present arrangements may serve the dominant—that is, the prevailing—interests of the present political system, but that does not mean that the majority of citizens are well served by them. If they are not, then no semireligious adulation of society's needs can be allowed to stand in the way of change. A society is simply a complex of human interrelationships with certain distinct patterns and a fairly definite boundary. Either of these elements can be transformed, partially or wholly, and the democratic creed would hold that they *should* be transformed when they get in the way of desired change. Societies are for people, quite simply, and not the other way around.

So who actually benefits? Only as we discover the answer to this question can we name and deal with the interest structure that is at the basis of the economic exploitation of women. It is clear that women do not benefit, neither the 37-odd million now on the labor market, the many millions more who would enter it if they had a chance, nor the innumerable others who are going to have to enter it sporadically or permanently in the years ahead. Neither are the children of these women better off because of the practice of discrimination. The low pay, the long hours, the lack of fringe benefits (child-care centers foremost among them)—all have the effect of making lives poorer, harder, and crueler, both for mothers and children. In 1974, 5.3 million children lived in poverty because their mothers, the main supporters of the family, could not get wages in their full-time jobs that would lift them above this level. Millions of others live in "near-poverty" because of the same situation.

At this time, it is far too easy an answer to point an accusing finger at men in general, for clearly, the husbands, the fathers, the brothers, and the sons of working women have at least a *material* interest in seeing the women of the family lift themselves up from their presently sorry socioeconomic state. It is also difficult to imagine a closely related male deliberately striving to deprive a woman of higher earnings and status that would be due her were she a man. To wish her to stay home, to express doubts in her ability and hostility to her ambition is quite another thing. Such attitudes have been inculcated in men—and in women as well—through the socialization process. But confronted with a working woman in the family, is it likely that a man would *actively* wish and work for her taking a back seat to male colleagues performing the same job? It could happen—and it no doubt has. One should be allowed to assume, however, that a good number of American men do not have to cling so precariously to their male egos that they cannot accept equality of opportunity for female family members, especially since their own economic burdens might be significantly lessened with such an arrangement. An insight into this possibility should be enough, were their humanitarian impulse to fail them, for them to accept the change.

But the common man does not, of course, have much to do with decisions to hire or to fire, to raise wages, and to create benefits for workers, whether male or female. Sex prejudice is pervasive, yes, but that does not mean everyone is equally responsible for the sexist differentiations on the labor market. It is to those empowered to make decisions we must look when we want change—*and when we want to find out why it hasn't taken place.*

We have defined woman as a consumer and as a seller of labor in the present economic system. We have also pointed to her marginal position, in the sense that she constitutes the greatest reserve labor force available in our society. This is of central importance for the comprehension of the interest structure underlying the web of discrimination on the job market, for the use of women as temporary workers, full- or part-time, is one of the most profitable arrangements available to employers in contemporary times. It is also a device to prevent any serious reordering of present structures and to allow the economy to expand and contract in response to new opportunities for the business elites and *not* in response to the needs of workers.

Take first the *extra profits* coming to employers because of the temporary status of many women workers and the comparatively lower earnings of all of them. Fringe benefits today are quite costly to the owners of business enterprises. Vacation pay, sick leave, extra medical benefits, contributions to pension plans—all of these can be avoided if employees stay at their job for only part of the day or part of the year—say, ninety days. This lesson has not been lost on the bosses of America. As economist Joan Jordan points out, it has become more and more common to maintain a skeleton crew of prime full-time workers, eliminating the young, the old, and the inexperienced women, and then to hire a supplementary crew of part-time workers.[21] Seasonal work is also increasing, as the time-study men in corporations are discovering its economic benefits. Layoff early in November, for instance, avoids extra pay for Veterans Day, Thanksgiving, Christmas, Washington's and Lincoln's birthdays, and whatever other holidays the workers have won guarantees of. Extra medical benefits and, of course, vacation pay are avoided by hiring women for three months in the summer. By cavalierly dismissing women workers with the rationalization that they are not the main breadwinners anyway, employers have the advantage of maintaining a floating crew of experienced labor at cheap rates, without having to take on any of the responsibilities and expenses that come their way by the maintenance of a full, regularly employed crew.

Ironically enough, these exploitative maneuvers often have the assistance of local unions. It is through them that the temporary hiring and firing is usually done. The ninety-day-or-less workers are asked to pay dues, too, under the illusion that they will be initiated into the union after a waiting period. But if they are laid off before initiation, they are not considered members and the dues are kept in the local, although the union has no obligation to find them jobs. Quite a windfall, as Joan Jordan comments, for the union officer who is more concerned with dues than with grievances![22] While it may appear to be a temporary gain for male union members in general, further reflection shows this to be a very shortsighted view. The use of women as a reserve labor force, just like the use of blacks for the same purpose, has the effect of making men more dispensable as well as of depressing wages for *all* groups on the grounds that if anyone prices himself or herself out of the market, replacements can easily be found. Present union members' desperate clinging to their security and advantages, with little or no regard for newcomers to the labor force, not only has prevented the expansion of the union movement in the last decades, but has also proven to be of little avail to long-time unionists as the economy constricts at the behest of business elites. Support for and loyalty to fellow workers, of both sexes, *might*, on the other hand,

[21]Joan Jordan, *The Place of American Women* (Boston: New England Free Press, 1969).
[22]Jordan, p. 5.

have put labor in the position to prevent such constriction. Greater in numbers and more superior in unity, the union movement would be in a much stronger position to make its claims upon the economic system. It must be kept in mind, after all, that ours is a system where scarcity of resources is no longer a basic problem; the question now is one of priorities for spending and not one of finding the economic means with which to keep everyone at work.[23]

The advantage, if any, to male union members of maintaining women workers in their present situation is at best of short duration and carries with it serious long-term costs. But to employers, the case for discrimination can be made easily enough. *The savings made possible by keeping women as a reserve labor force, although considerable, are as nothing compared to the profits to be had by continuing the lower wages offered women for work identical to that performed by men.* Some employers are even honest about it, reveals Lyn Wells. One of them replied, during the Conference on Equal Pay in 1952, when asked why the pay of women in his factory was less than that of men: "Tradition, I suppose. . . . Anyhow, it's cheaper."[24]

Exactly how much cheaper the arrangement may be is suggested in an early study by economist Grace Hutchins. Using Census reports and figures from the Securities and Exchange Commission, she calculates that in 1950 manufacturing companies realized profits of $5.4 billion by paying women less per year than men for similar work.[25] The extra profits extracted in this way formed 23 percent of all company profits that year. The Equal Pay Act, requiring equal pay for equal work, has been in existence since 1963. Yet violations are still frequent and serious; it often takes lawsuits to bring about approximate enforcements. In 1974 it was found that nearly 33,000 employees had been underpaid by more than $20.6 million as a result of such litigation. Nearly all these employees were women.[26]

To know *where* women work is also of importance for the full

[23]See, for example, J. K. Galbraith's analysis in *The Affluent Society* (Boston: Houghton Mifflin, 1958).

[24]Lyn Wells, *American Women: Their Use and Abuse* (Boston: New England Free Press, 1969), p. 9.

[25]Grace Hutchins, *Women Who Work* (New York: International Publishers, 1952), p. 9.

[26]Citizens' Advisory Council on the Status of Women, *Women in 1974* (Washington, D.C., 1975), p. 7

comprehension of the interest structure maintained by their sub-
jugation. Industries that are highly automated and enjoy nearly
monopolistic control in their area of production have less of a need
to control wages than do industries that are labor-intensive. In the
former, higher wages are simply passed on to the consumer in the
form of higher prices—with no effective government controls,
labor costs are not allowed to affect profits. But in industries with
low rates of automation, such as the textile and clothing industries,
substantially higher wages would mean not just less profit but a
transformation or demise of the enterprise. In textiles, for instance, it might force automation, if the industry is to survive the
competition from abroad. How this bears on the problem of
women is brilliantly shown by Peggy Morton. The industries with
the lowest rate of automation are also those who employ the greater
number of women. About 70 percent of women workers are in the
textile, clothing, and related industries, in food and beverages, or
in electrical appliances or supplies. How crucial are the savings to
be had from the lower wages paid women is amply illustrated by a
comparison of average weekly wages in 1969: for clothing and
related industries, where women workers dominate, they were $78
and in leather products $81; whereas in chemicals and nonmetallic
leather products, where women make up only 22 percent and 11
percent of the workers respectively, the wages were $139 and
$133.[27]

But more women are, of course, employed in the service sector
than in manufacturing. Work here is most often uncreative and
tedious, working conditions are bad, and economic rewards are
minimal. A good part of the women here belong to the "economic
underworld," as Michael Harrington aptly names it,[28] financially
backward, immune to progress, incredibly capable of being exploited. Unions are kept out, by and large, and when allowed in, it
is the labor racketeers who are invited to make deals without any of
the standard provisions for wage rates, fringe benefits, and so forth
of honest union contracts. The shortsightedness of labor leaders is
again to be blamed: it is the AFL-CIO "no raiding" agreement that
makes this possible. Once a racket local has a charter in a recog-

---

[27]Peggy Morton, "A Woman's Work Is Never Done," *Leviathan* 2, no. 1 (May
1970): 32–38.
[28]Michael Harrington, *The Other America* (New York: Macmillan, 1963), p. 26.

nized international, honest unions are stopped from going in to take over from the crooks. And again, the arrangement causes more women than men to suffer. Unions have been notably lax in extending their protection to women: only one out of seven women workers belongs to a union; for men the ratio is one out of four.

Wages in the economic underworld reflect the unprotected state of women workers. Chambermaids in hotels got only $2.35 in average hourly wages in 1973. In laundry and cleaning services, where women constituted slightly more than three-fourths of the non-supervisory personnel, the average earnings were $2.50 per hour in 1973. Conditions are similar among service workers in hospitals—also mainly women.[29]

It stands to reason that *such low wages could not easily be offered to major groups of male workers today.* Neither is it likely that legislators on both federal and state levels would persist in their resistance to extend coverage of the minimum-wage laws to such occupations were the workers affected mainly men. If millions of men rather than millions of women had to endure the low salaries and unprotected status of these professions, there would soon enough be grumblings, protests, organization, and strikes. But women are different, aren't they? Nonaggressive, nonambitious, preferring really to be homemakers, they also do not need to earn as much as men. Or so it is believed.

Only the secondary status of women in American society and their exclusion from the major centers of power could make possible such continued and severe exploitation of a major portion of the labor force. Those who benefit are, as has been shown, the business elites and no others.

[29]Elizabeth Waldman and Beverly J. McEaddy, "Where Women Work," *Monthly Labor Review*, May 1974, p. 3.

four

Power and the American Woman

The racism analogy holds up exceedingly well when applied to the problems of women on the job market. Women do indeed constitute a minority in the sociological sense, the largest and yet most exploited of all minorities in the labor force. It will no longer do, as has been pointed out, to rationalize the sex gap by insisting that women are basically homemakers. Like it or not, 37 million of them are wage earners, 14 million self-supporting, and 7 million providing for their families as well. For the rest, work is often an economic necessity because of the low incomes of their husbands, not to speak of the instability of the institution of marriage. In spite of the fact that women, in Helen Hacker's ironic comment, are the only minority in history that lives with the master race,[1] it makes sense to define the position of women employees in the stratification system separately from the positions of their husbands or fathers. And when we do, it becomes clear that by far the majority of women working today belong with the working class in terms of salaries, benefits, and opportunities enjoyed.

As a working-class minority, women do, however, have possession of one resource that has the potential for power inherent in it, especially given the number of individuals involved here. That resource is *political*—citizenship or full membership in the political class. Were it not for this important right, shared equally with men,

[1]Helen Hacker, "Women as a Minority Group," *Social Forces*, no. 3 (1951): 7.

working women might be most accurately designated as an "under class," "a group without influence, subject to manipulation, and without legitimate means for redressing grievances."[2] The first two parts of the definition certainly fit. But then, women *do* have the vote. And the vote does, in fact, give them more than a "legitimate means" for redressing grievances; it provides them with a potential power base of great significance, given their superior numbers both in the nation and in the voting populace, for women constituted no less than 53.3 percent of eligible voters as of July 1970.[3]

Citizenship is one resource that—in a democracy—is equally distributed. It does not divide the nation into "haves" and "have-nots." It can, quite to the contrary, be used by the latter to change the relationships in the distribution of goods and services in a society, for it is government that is the central agency for the authoritative allocation of resources and it is by effective use of the vote that a group or a coalition of groups can capture whole or partial control of the governmental machinery. Democracy's advantage and attractiveness as a governmental system stems in large part from its potential in this area. The one resource shared equally by all adult members of the society *may* be used by the socially and economically underprivileged to upset the status quo and to change the distributive pattern in existence at any time. The tables can be turned in the conflict between the "haves" and "have-nots" when—and only when—the government becomes involved on behalf of those disadvantaged. *Numbers,* translated into *votes,* make the difference—numbers sufficient to put in office those who will act on behalf of groups of citizens exercising their democratic prerogative. Women are not only on a par with, they have it over, men in terms of *potential* for obtaining political power. *Why* is it, then, that their resources in this important sphere have not been translated into rights and benefits so sorely lacking for working women?

Equal pay, job opportunities, Social Security, employment insurance, and other benefits are but some of the issues of great significance to citizens in a weak socioeconomic position. In the past it is to government that they have turned, nearly all of them, to get their due or to obtain the rights necessary to seek satisfaction for

[2]Louis Knowles and Kenneth Prewitt, *Institutional Racism in America* (Englewood Cliffs, N.J.: Prentice-Hall, 1969), p. 165.

[3]*Congressional Record,* July 10, 1970, p. 1745.

their needs. Every impoverished and subordinated group in America tends to follow this course of action, be it the small farmers, the laborers, the blacks, or the farmworkers. Invariably, their fight to gain a greater measure of justice comes to focus on the need to get the government on their side. Consider what the social landscape in America might be without the limit on working hours, without Social Security, without the Wagner Act, without the minimum wage, or without civil rights legislation. It is certain that it would be a different scene, and it is probable that it would be a much uglier one!

So what happened in regard to women? For more than half a century now women have enjoyed formal political rights on an equal basis with men. It is clear that this formidable weapon, full membership in the political class, has been of little or no use to this majority in terms of gaining equal rights and opportunities for the 44 percent of it now in the labor force. Even if one were to hypothesize a dichotomy of interests between women who work and women who don't work, the sheer numbers of the former, 37 million as of 1975, would be quite enough to make a tremendous political impact on legislation and rule making in a system characterized by group politics—provided, of course, that they are *seen* as an actual or potential group by the present lawmakers and provided that they, *as a group,* have representation in legislative councils and governmental agencies. But *that,* of course, entails something more than and different from a right to vote.

We have come to recognize, in viewing the struggle of blacks to gain their share of the American pie, that the mere possession of citizenship means precious little indeed for those left out of the mainstream. Blacks have been able to vote not just for a half, but for a whole century and are still intensely involved in the fight to translate this essential resource into calculable and concrete social advantages. In the process, they have had to go through several distinct stages of legal action, of extra legal political activity, of self-exploration, of gaining recognition—all with the ultimate aim of organizing a political power base. The vote has to be used, first of all. The voters have to be unified on the crucial issues, pressure has to be applied on decision makers at all levels, representatives have to be found to articulate and push through the demands of black citizens. Without such a power base, without representatives on the decision-making levels within political institutions, citizenship remains but a potential and not an actual resource for groups that are socially and economically disadvantaged.[4] The focus in the civil rights movement is increasingly on electing representatives to legislative bodies and seeking top administrative positions for individuals who can be relied on to act in the interest of the black minority. That such individuals might be nonblack is a possibility that is still disputed in the black community. What is uniformly recognized, however, is that black citizens are likely to gain a fairer and more effective representation if they capture for their own group members the maximum possible share of decision-making posts. To "get one's own people up there" is a desire that is as familiar as it is rational in societies where public representatives are entrusted with the authoritative allocation of scarce resources.

With this in mind, let us then take a realistic look at the political power base possessed by women in this country. They have the vote—OK. But of what use has it been up to now? What, for instance, is women's share of positions in legislatures, on top administrative levels, in city councils, on boards of supervisors and boards of education—in any and all of the institutions where membership presumably opens the way for equal and/or effective representation? Is their part of political power in these very real terms as negligible as the advances made by women in the occupational field? If so, then the latter situation is at least partially explained.

We shall, for the moment, proceed in this investigation on the assumption that there is a politically significant relationship between the proportion of representative positions a group can claim for itself and the degree to which the needs and interests of that group are articulated and acted upon in political institutions.[5] That

[4]This has been most convincingly demonstrated in the works of T. H. Marshall, the British sociologist—for example, *Citizenship and Social Class* (London: Cambridge University Press, 1950); and by E. E. Schattschneider, American political scientist, in *The Semi-Sovereign People* (New York: Holt, Rinehart and Winston, 1960).

[5]The concept of representation is as complex as it is elusive. It should be made clear that I accept the definition offered by Hanna Pitkin that representation means acting in the interest of the represented, in a manner responsive to them. See Hanna T. Pitkin, *The Concept of Representation* (Berkeley: University of California Press, 1967), p. 209. This interpretation does not *require* that a representative of a group be a member by birth, religion, or class affiliation of the same group. It is considered likely, however, that the more group members are in decision-making positions, the better chance the group has of fair and effective representation.

For provocative exploration into the meaning of representation to democratic governance, see also Heinz Eulau and Kenneth Prewitt, "Political Matrix and Political Representation: Prolegomenon to a New Departure from an Old Problem," *American Political Science Review* 63, no. 2 (June 1969): 427–42.

the relationship is not exact is evident enough: the proportion of workers elected or selected to decision-making positions in government is shockingly low, yet much legislation and rule making benefiting workers has come through in recent decades.[6] It is clear, on the other hand, that the continued social and economic privileges of the business and professional class are in no small measure due to their striking overrepresentation in legislative councils. In societies where members of the working class have captured for themselves a fairer proportion of decision-making positions, the degree of social and economic inequality has been significantly reduced.

How do women fare, then? Are they to be found on the very bottom of the stratification system in terms of *this* resource— political power—just as they are in regard to the other vital resources already examined?

The Washington Power Base

We can start by looking at women's share of elective and appointive offices in the federal government.

The central position of the presidency in the American power structure is recognized by all scholars in the field. Yet none has cared to speculate on the anomaly that not one representative of the majority has been even seriously considered for this all-important office. Congresswoman Shirley Chisholm (D., N.Y.) ran a brave and resourceful campaign for her party's nomination in 1972, but fell far short of winning in spite of the enthusiasm of her supporters. In 1976 no woman tried.

Worse than this, even the vice-presidential slot still is ruled out-of-bounds for women candidates. While the talented Sissy Fahrenholt of Texas came close to winning her party's nomination in 1972, that near-coup was considered as much due to the volatile political atmosphere of an unusual convention as to the strong qualifications of the candidate. As late as 1976 the National Women's Political Caucus and the Democratic Women's Agenda

[6]In the period 1947–57 skilled and unskilled labor had only two representatives in Congress. In fact, government officials generally are recruited from the well-educated and affluent upper and upper-middle classes. See Donald Matthews, *Social Background of Political Decision Makers* (New York: Doubleday, 1954). See also U.S. Bureau of the Census, *Historical Statistics of the U.S.* (Washington, D.C.: U.S. Government Printing Office, 1962).

met with defeat in trying to promote a woman candidate for vice-president. Congresswoman Barbara Jordan was their choice after her spellbinding introductory speech at the convention. Ms. Jordan—realistic as always—refused the nomination. "I don't have much interest in being a symbol," she said. "Maybe in another four years. . . . We're still trying to get the country ready."[7]

But the resistance to women entering the presidential races in the seventies cannot be viewed as simply a consequence of making *victory* the first priority on the part of power wielders within either party. A sharp increase in support for a woman president was demonstrated by a Gallup Poll in the fall of 1975. Given the finding that seven out of ten Americans believed the nation would be governed as well or better if a woman were president, the public in this case seems to be ahead of the kingmakers of either major party.

The highlights in the thirty-eight-year trend in support of a woman president are worth noting. As shown in Table 4.1, the Gallup organization reported the sharpest rise in that support after the advent of "Women's Liberation."

TABLE 4.1   Proportion of People Believing a
Woman Capable of Being President

Year	Yes	No	No Opinion
1975	73%	28%	4%
1971	66	29	5
1969	54	39	7
1955	52	44	4
1949	48	48	4
1937	31	65	4

Source: Reported in the *San Francisco Examiner*, September 18, 1975, p. 22.

The change in sentiment on the part of the public is by no means correlated to any advance of women into national offices. Their share of representation in Congress, for example, remains shockingly low as late as 1976.

In the Senate the lone woman holdout, Margaret Chase Smith

[7]*Washington Post*, July 16, 1976, p. 5.

(R., Maine), lost her bid for reelection in 1972, and that most august chamber on Capitol Hill was again free of female voices. In all, only ten women have served the Senate since 1920, and access for these chosen few was gained most often because they happened to be widows of successful officeholders. Their parties offered them nomination not out of desire to open up the field to women, but in order to capitalize on the goodwill generated by the late husband, to gain the sympathy vote, or to prevent a general contest for the office. As Martin Gruberg points out, before the successful and courageous Claire Booth Luce was elected to office in 1942, almost all female legislators in Washington, D.C., had been either single or widows.[8]

The United States also went into its bicentennial celebration with its female half of the citizenry having achieved only 4.1% representation in Congress. Nineteen congresswomen at this time shared power—in the formal sense—with 417 congressmen. If we were to have women representatives in this key legislative body in rough proportion to the number of eligible women voters, there would instead be 220 congresswomen and 215 congressmen. In the upper house, moreover, there would be 51 women senators and 49 men senators. Unthinkable? Indeed—yet the question is, *why so?*

But the political power of representatives has to be measured by criteria other than the mere holding of office. The ability to initiate and to amend legislation, the right and opportunity to take part in the investigative function of Congress, the influence over budget appropriations, the ability, ultimately, to give legislative help to one's constituents—all of this depends on the representative's committee assignments. The power hierarchy within both houses, supported by protocol, the committee and seniority systems, and the "informal folkways" of Washington, totally dominates the legislative arena. Without assignment to one of the prestigious committees and the ear and/or sympathy, if not the possession, of the chairmanship, the power of an individual member of Congress is significantly reduced. And if, in addition to the lack of "juicy" committee assignments, a representative does not gain access to and inclusion in the tangled web of informal and semistructured

---

[8]Martin Gruberg, *Women in Politics: A Source Book* (New York: Academic Press, 1968), p. 121.

relationships of power wielders and influentials, he or she might as well forget about leaving an imprint on the legislation coming out of the nation's capital.

How do women representatives in Congress measure up when judged in terms of these criteria of power? The answer reveals itself easily enough as we examine their terms in office, their committee assignments, and their inclusion in the informal small groups of congressional leaders and intimates.

First, let us look at women's longevity in congressional offices. A freshman representative, it is customarily admitted, is unlikely to exercise any influence over public policy. Congressman Everett G. Burkhalter of California offered a succinct and revealing commentary on the situation in 1964. Explaining why he did not seek re-election, the sixty-seven-year-old representative said: "I could see I was not going to get any place. Nobody listens to what you have to say until you have been there 10 or 12 years. These old men have everything so tied down you can't do anything. There are only about 40 out of the 435 members who call the shots. They're the committee chairmen and the ranking members and they're all around 70 or 80."[9]

Of the sixty-five women who had served in Congress up to 1968, twenty-four stayed at the job *no more than one term or less.* Another sixteen served two terms and another seven served three. Only twenty-two congresswomen in the first fifty years after winning the vote had been in office four or more terms. It is widely accepted that it is not until the fourth term—and sometimes later—that a representative gains the recognition and influence among peers that she or he needs to be an effective legislator.

What about committee assignments and chairmanships? As Professor Frieda Geblen points out, women representatives have over the years been assigned disproportionally to the lesser-status committees.[10] A survey of the congressional establishment in the Ninety-fourth Congress (first session, 1975) more than confirms her conclusions. First of all, no women were included in the House leadership—Speaker, majority leader and whip, minority leader

[9]Quoted in Thomas R. Dye and L. Harmon Zeigler, *The Irony of Democracy* (Belmont, Calif.: Wadsworth, 1970), p. 247.

[10]Frieda Geblen, "Women in Congress," *Trans-Action,* October 1969, p. 37.

and whip, caucus or conference chairs. In the prestigious and powerful committees of the House, the participation of women was as follows:

> Rules—No women (16 men)
> Ways and Means—1 woman (Martha Keys, D., Kans.) of 37 members
> Interstate and Foreign Commerce—No women (43 men)
> Judiciary—2 women (Barbara Jordan, D., Tex., and Elizabeth Holtzman, D., N.Y.) of 37 members
> Government Operations—2 women (Bella S. Abzug, D., N.Y., and Barbara Jordan, D., Tex.) among 43 members
> Foreign Affairs—1 woman (Helen S. Meyner, D., N.J.) among 37 members
> Banking and Currency—2 women (Lindy Boggs, D., La., and Gladys Noon Spellman, D., Md.) among 43 members
> Armed Services—2 women (Patricia Schroeder, D., Colo., and Marjorie S. Holt, R., Md.) among 40 members
> Appropriations—1 woman (Yvonne Braithwaite Burke, D., Calif.) among 55 members
> Agriculture—1 woman (Margaret M. Heckler, R., Mass.) among 43 members
>
> *Source: Congressional Directory* (1975).

We find, in the end, that one woman has been elevated to the chairmanship of a committee. She is Leonor K. Sullivan (D., Mo.), but—as is predictable by now—her assignment is not one endowed with great status or power: the Merchant Marine and Fisheries Committee.

When it comes to the *informal relationships* so crucial to the successful maneuvering and power play within Congress, indications are strong that women are, again, virtually excluded. What goes on in the men's clubs and bars, on golf courses, and in gyms can be of great significance in terms of exchange of information, nurturing of friendships, swapping of confidences and promises. The fact is that women are simply not invited to and not particularly welcome in these informal gatherings. Middle-class mores, male chauvinism, quaint chivalry—any or all characteristics contribute to their exclusion. How complete and how devastating this can be is indicated in the remarks of a male administrative aide to one of the congresswomen:

No woman can ever make it. The power structure doesn't operate that way. So much of the power structure is built around the golf course, the bar, over cards, in the gym shower room, etc. I doubt that the best or most able of women can ever get into the inner circle where there is complete acceptance. There are always some differences. Particularly is this true among Southerners; she is not accepted there as an equal. Where the men may banter and tease about an issue—"Hey Joe, what do you mean by adding that amendment; trying to break the country?" sort of thing—with her they just say, "Why, certainly, Mrs. Blank, I'll think about it." But they don't. They give deference, but they don't give any real attention.[11]

Who else has power in the federal government? There is, of course, the president's cabinet. Appointive offices all, here *might* be an arena where the recognition of women's needs and abilities is not inhibited too much by the possible prejudice of the greater public. The president, as the leader of all the people and the spokesman of the whole nation, could surely be expected to take cognizance of the fact that women now have full political membership in this country—and a potential majority of votes as well. One might expect that his appointments—to the cabinet and to other high offices—reflect this reality, by now more than a half-century old.

But no. Up to the mid-seventies only three women have held cabinet rank in the federal government. The first two were Frances Perkins, secretary of labor from 1933 to 1945, and Oveta Culp Hobby, secretary of health, education, and welfare from 1953 to 1955. Neither the liberal President Kennedy, the reportedly pro-woman President Johnson, nor the professedly fair-minded President Nixon found it opportune to select one member of the majority group in this nation to serve in their cabinets. President Ford finally broke the mold by appointing Carla A. Hills as secretary of housing and urban development in the fall of 1974.

Women do fare better in lower-level appointive offices, it is true—just a *little* better. In the foreign service, for example, all of ten women had served as ambassadors and ministers between 1920 and 1970. The foreign service in an earlier study was shown to have 3,061 women among a total of 10,769 employees. Among foreign

[11]Geblen, p. 39.

service officers, however, women constituted less than one-tenth of the total.[12]

But women appear to be doing well in the foreign service compared with other branches of the federal government. Of the 671,150 women in the full-time federal white-collar work force in October 1972—33.7 percent of the total—only 193 held the top positions, grades GS-16 through GS-18. All of 10,261 were at these supergrade levels at the same time, and that means women constituted *only 1.9 percent* of the total here.[13]

The U.S. Postal Service offers a striking example of the limited mobility of women in a branch of the federal government where women have always made up a significant portion of the work force (about one-fourth). Only 6 women employed here (among 122,938) earned salaries above $25,000. By comparison, 700 men had earnings in this category, and 128 took home a paycheck between $30,000 and $40,000—a category that *no* women were found in.[14]

In the judicial branch of the federal government, *no* women are found in positions above the rank of 13, and in the Department of Justice only 3 women made it into rank 16 and 2 women into rank 17. By comparison, again, all of 409 men had reached this level in the department in 1971.[15]

There is no need, of course, to elaborate on the absence of women on the Supreme Court. Not only has no woman been selected to serve in that crucially important body, but none of the "fair sex"—the majority of citizens—have even been seriously considered for the office. Among district court justices in 1972, we find only 4 women, moreover—of a total of 399.

In 1975 the Citizens' Advisory Council on the Status of Women took note that in the governing bodies of three key organizations dealing with the media, only one woman was included: no women were found in top management positions either in the Federal

[12]U.S. Civil Service Commission, Statistics Section, *Study of Employment of Women in the Federal Government, 1967* (Washington, D.C.; U.S. Government Printing Office, 1968).

[13]Bureau of Manpower Information Systems, *Federal Civilian Employment: Women* (Washington D.C., 1973).

[14]Bureau of Manpower Information Systems.

[15]Bureau of Manpower Information Systems.

Communications Commission, the Corporation for Public Broadcasting, or the Federal Trade Commission. After study and discussion of the inaccurate manner in which women are portrayed by the public media, the Advisory Council recommended that more women with demonstrated commitment to constructive change be appointed to all three bodies.[16]

The dismal record of women's share of decision-making positions in the legislative arena is not even matched, then, by their share of power in the executive and judicial branches of the federal government. The virtual absense of women in top positions in these areas, positions that carry with them the responsibilities, the access, and the prestige that guarantee influence and/or authority, provides overwhelming evidence of women's lack of representation in the nation's political power structure. Vote or no vote, as far as formal power in the federal government is concerned, women just have not made any breakthrough yet.

The State Capitals: Another Male World

Can the picture be improved upon by looking at the legislative and executive positions within state and local governments? Or are women once more to be found outside the main arena where influence is brought to bear, decisions made, and public policies implemented?

Again, the scene is quite easily surveyed. And again, women are notable for their absence and not their presence.

The most important office on the state level is, generally speaking, the governorship. The record shows that only four women have succeeded in being elected governor since women got the chance to run for and elect candidates to this exclusive position. The first three of them, moreover, owe their success to something other than recognition of their own personal assets and/or the right and fairness of electing a member of the majority to this office. Each of them succeeded husbands who had held the post before them, and in the case of two out of the three, it was widely recognized that they ran in lieu of their husbands, who promised to and did run the administration for them.

[16]Citizens' Advisory Council on the Status of Women, *Women in 1974.*

In the case of Miriam A. ("Ma") Ferguson of Texas, her husband, a former governor, had been impeached and was therefore disqualified from running for office. Ma Ferguson, whose husband had disapproved of the women's rights movement, was in office from 1924 to 1926 and again from 1932 to 1936. Her campaign slogan was "Two governors for the price of one."[17] Lurleen Wallace of Alabama was the other woman to stand in for a husband frustrated in his desire to run for the governorship. It was only when Governor George Wallace failed in his attempt to change the state constitution to permit his reelection in 1966 that he put up his wife as the nominal candidate for the office he wanted for himself. The campaign made it very clear that a vote for her would be a vote for him. It made for an easy victory. Lurleen Wallace's short and dependent career ended with her death before her first term in office was over.

The third woman governor in the history of the United States, Nellie Taylor Ross of Wyoming, did not even do any campaigning when she was elected in 1925 to fill the unexpired term of her husband. Being in mourning and having no political experience, she left all that to her male campaign manager. Her victory, one presumes, had more to do with sympathy and nostalgia than with any faith in the female candidate.

A significant victory for women was finally scored in 1974 when Ella Grasso was elected to be the new governor of Connecticut. A veteran of the party and past campaigns, her victory was very much her own. Though Ella Grasso is not regarded as a committed feminist, women throughout the state and nation took an interest in the race and most feminists rejoiced in the election.

The importance of the resurgence of the new feminism is also attested to by the fact that 1974 was also the first year women in any numbers were elected to important state offices. The National Women's Political Caucus reports: "Women newly elected to offices like Secretary of State, State Treasurer, Auditor and Superintendent of Public Instruction show an increase of 36 percent over the last election year."[18]

A quick survey of these offices reveals, however, how much further women have yet to go before attaining anything near equity

[17]Gruberg, *Women in Politics*, pp. 189–90.
[18]Quoted in Citizens' Advisory Council on the Status of Women, *Women in 1974*.

with men in important offices in state government. Only one woman, Mary Ann Krupsak in New York, was elected to be lieutenant governor—an office to which accrues a significant amount of independent power and prestige. Eight women, on the other hand, won election as secretary of state: in Alabama, California, Connecticut, Kansas, Minnesota, New Mexico, South Dakota, and Wyoming. A potentially influential position, the secretary of state office is not usually considered a key one in the state power structure. This is even more true for the position of treasurer, to which seven women were elected in 1974. A significant break-through came, however, with the election of Carolyn Warner to superintendent of public instruction in Arizona. The estimate from the National Women's Political Caucus is that women held forty-five statewide elective offices in 1975. Of these, it should be noted, all of thirty-one were elected in 1974.

In the social policy area, it is, of course, the state legislatures that are most important. Representation in these bodies is important for anyone with a stake in decisions affecting education, law enforce-ment, crime prevention, health, welfare, housing, and other areas of prime public concern. State and local governments consistently spend more on such domestic programs than does the federal gov-ernment. The noise and clamor of lobbies and interest groups in every state legislature in the nation are a telling indication of the importance attached to the decision-making power of the incum-bents.

The issues dealt with by state legislatures are also of the type that women are presumed to have a greater interest in. Their degree of success in breaking into this sector of the male power structure is therefore of special interest at this time. How well do they do?

The answer is—and it is becoming almost repetitious at this point—not very well, not very well at all! Though encouraging gains were made in the number of women holding state offices in the early seventies, it should be emphasized that they are still very far from having obtained their fair share of representation. In 1967 women held only 318 out of 7,700 legislative seats on the state level. Their numbers steadily increased in the four following elections—again corresponding to the advent of Women's Liberation—until in 1975 women counted 610 among the nation's state legislators. Note, however, that though this signifies an increase of 80 percent, women's share of representation still was only 8 percent on the state level in the mid-seventies.[19]

Looking at the power structure within state legislatures, the impression of an overwhelmingly male world is further confirmed. No more than five women have acted as floor leaders for their respective parties, and only three as Speakers of the state lower house. A mere three women have acted as presidents pro tem of the upper houses.[20] The lack of advancement for women into these formal positions of leadership is of special importance, since it is through these offices that the much-disputed and all-important committee assignments are handled. Viewed in the light of the great weight given to informal relationships, another area in which women are greatly handicapped, the absence of women on this top level takes on added significance.

The Politics Closest to Home

Are things any better, then, in the government that is "closest to home"—on the local level?

Surprisingly, the answer is no. At the county level—where "women's issues" of health, education, and welfare figure very prominently—we find that in 1975 women's share of representation was considerably lower than it was on the state level, and lower even than it was in Congress. Out of 17,000 elected county commissioners only 400 were women. That comes out to slightly above 2 percent! On the city level, women fare better: 4,400 were city councilpersons out of a potential number of 134,000 such elected officials in 1974. And in that same year 550 women could be counted as mayors, though only two held that office in major American cities (Oklahoma City, Oklahoma, and San Jose, California).

The great numbers of women rumored to be moving into city and county posts[21] are quite simply not to be found in the positions to which power is attached. It is as library board members, treasurers, treasury clerks, and finance commissioners that women have

[19]Data from the recent elections come from the National Women's Political Caucus.

[20]Gruberg, *Women in Politics,* pp. 179–81.

[21]Gruberg, p. 201.

found their way into governmental councils to any significant degree. Moreover, their still limited success in these areas can be attributed largely to two factors: (1) such local positions are often part-time and poorly paid and there are comparatively few men who seek them; and (2) given the nonpartisan character of these local offices, they are considered "more suitable for the ladies" than the competitive and power-invested posts on other levels of government.

One important elective position presumably more open to women and—one may presume—of special interest to them as mothers and as teachers is that of school board member. This is an important post in any community. It is, after all, through the school boards that the school budget is dispersed, educational standards set, curricula and teachers approved. The potential for power here is obvious—such decisions have direct bearing on shaping the minds of the young, influencing not just their careers, but their very life styles. Strikingly, women amount to no more than 9.7 percent of the school board members in the nation, according to the National School Board Association. More than half of the boards reported they had no women members at all. Of the remaining half, only twelve had more than one woman sitting as a member. Here, it appears that only in the big cities have women gained acceptance in a field of policy making they would seem eminently suited to. Women constitute 23 percent of big-city school boards.[22]

And so the picture is complete. In terms of formal political power, in terms of their proportionate share of representation on the decision-making levels in federal, state, and local government, women are left out or take a back seat even more systematically and dramatically than in the socioeconomic realm. The presumed "power" of the American woman turns out to be a myth—if anything, a greater myth than the stereotyped belief that the American woman is secure, pampered, and spoiled in this best of all worlds—for females.

"Women's Vote"

One question comes immediately to mind in reviewing the dis-

[22]Gruberg, p. 215.

mal· record of women's share of political power. Is it because women are less active in politics that they do so poorly for themselves?

First, let us look at women's choices at the polls. There has always been and still is some difference in the voting activity of men and women, and every major election will turn up speculations about and jocular references to the "women's vote" by party pros and observers of the scene. Women are supposed to be more candidate-oriented than men, more easily impressed by the apparent virility and good looks of male candidates, and less rational —that is, less interest-oriented—in their choices than are men. The evidence for these assertions is by and large unimpressive— unexamined assumptions and tired old chichés seem to be of the essence in most. As to the male sex appeal supposedly influencing women voters, Clare Williams, a former director of the Women's Division of the National Republican Committee, has the following retort: "If Marilyn Monroe was running against Eleanor Roosevelt, I suppose some men would be influenced, too." She adds, "I don't feel that Bob Taft was a handsome man, yet women rallied behind him fervently."[23]

Her Democratic counterpart, Katie Louchheim, is equally firm in rejecting the theory: "If there is any secret to reveal about dealing with women it is that . . . they cannot be won over by virile masculine smiles, honeyed compliments, and precious prose. In 1944, Wendell Willkie was a fine figure of a man, but look what the Republicans did—they threw him out for the little man on the wedding cake."[24] And the wedding-cake man (Thomas E. Dewey), one might add, also went down to defeat in a later contest with crusty old Harry Truman, at that time hardly distinguished either by sex appeal or by the "fatherly image" said to attract women to Dwight D. Eisenhower.

What serious research findings we have point to slight, but potent, differences and will be discussed in the context of socialization processes and male and female roles in our society. Any review of policy outcome, however, makes it clear that *if* there is a women's vote, it certainly has not been put to use on behalf of women. As for

[23]Quoted in Sidney Shalett, "Is There a Women's Vote?" *Saturday Evening Post,* September 17, 1960, p. 80.
[24]Quoted in Shalett, p. 80.

partisan preference of female voters, these do not, as Professor Warren Miller concludes, differ markedly from those of men.[25]

Neither, it turns out, are there any significant differences between the voting ratios of men and women. In fact, the differences have been gradually reduced in recent years to the point where in the 1968 election, the turnout of women of voting age was 64 percent and of men 67.8 percent.[26] A very slight gap, indeed. Certainly, it is as nothing compared to the veritable gulf in representation between the two sexes in the political arena.

Since women vote in very nearly as great numbers as men, then, can their lack of representation in governmental councils be explained by their abstinence from party politics and campaign activities? No, not as far as effort is concerned. The mere suggestion of such a cause is laughable to anyone remotely familiar with political campaigns and the role of volunteers in them. Were it not for the willing and hard-working women throwing themselves into the "nitty-gritty" of campaign activities and maintenance of volunteer organizations, it is a fair bet that the present party structures would quickly come to a point of collapse. Very few candidates would be so rash and foolish as the Republican congressman who cavalierly dismissed women willing to work their fingers to the bone for his reelection: "Well, girls, don't get too upset about it," he is reported to have told them. "My organization is running smoothly, so don't you worry your pretty little heads." The "girls" didn't, according to Clare Williams, and the congressman went down to defeat against a candidate with a less patronizing attitude toward women.[27] It is worth noting that it was not just the general preference by women for the Eisenhower candidacy that made his victory a landslide, but the fact that about 6 million women volunteers were reported to have worked eagerly in his campaign.[28]

Reluctant and strangely fearful recognition was given to women party workers by a prominent male activist some years ago. Wrote John Fischer, editor of *Harper's* magazine: "Note who actually does the political work in your own community. Who is it that sells

[25]Quoted in Shalett, p. 81.

[26]U.S. Bureau of the Census, *Statistical Abstracts of the United States, 1969* (1969), table 536, p. 371.

[27]Shalett, "Is There a Women's Vote?" p. 80.

[28]Shalett, p. 80.

tickets to the Annual Dinner, mails out reminders to register, gives tea parties for the Peerless Leaders, keeps minutes at committee meetings, drives voters to the polls on election day? Nine times out of ten a woman. The insidious fact is that they work harder."[29]

What is *insidious* about it, according to John Fischer, is that one day they might just take over. He waxes positively lyrical in conjuring up this abhorrent spectacle:

> One of these mornings all of the district leaders in the country will stroll down to their club rooms, chomping their cigars without a worry in the world. When they open their doors they will find the windows have been swathed in pastel curtains, the spittoons and pinochle decks thrown out, the poker layouts converted into vanity tables, and all those cracked and cherished leather chairs draped in chintz. And if they don't like it, the ladies will be ready and able to elect a bunch of Ardent Amateurs to take their place. It's later than you think.[30]

It turned out that John Fischer and other male defenders of the fort had little to fear, after all. As of 1970, women were no closer to the reins of power in politics than they were in the mid-fifties. But the attitude toward women in politics revealed by this prominent liberal intellectual is by no means atypical. Women in politics still tend to be typed as "fluttery females—or bespectacled battleaxes," as Katie Louchheim protested in 1960.[31]

The prevailing pattern in party politics is now, as then, to encourage "the girls" to come out and work in campaigns and generally to rely on them for volunteer clerical services, but to give them a cold and even hostile shoulder if they have ambitions beyond that. This is the norm, according to a number of women who made it against the odds.[32] India Edwards, for many years the vice-chairman of the Democratic National Committee, reports: "If the party backs a woman you can be pretty sure they do it because they

---

[29]Quoted in Marian V. Sanders, *The Lady and the Vote* (Boston: Houghton Mifflin, 1956), p. 31.

[30]Quoted in Sanders, *The Lady and the Vote*, p. 54.

[31]Quoted in Shalett, "Is There a Women's Vote?" p. 80.

[32]Senator Margaret Chase Smith and Representatives Margaret Heckler, Marian Sanders, Kate Louchheim, and Clare Williams are but some of the women politicos who have talked of the resistance of party bigwigs to their career plans. Three of the eight prominent women discussed in Peggy Lawson's *Few Are Chosen* (Boston: Houghton Mifflin, 1968), p. xxiii, had to run for office without party endorsement.

think it is a lost cause but they know they have to have *some* candidate." Her observation is cheerfully affirmed by John Bailey, former national chairman of the Democratic party: "The only time to run a woman is when things look so bad that your only chance is to do something dramatic."[33] And Clare Williams tells of a certain county chairman's reluctant sanction of the first woman candidate of his party to run for Congress in his district. His admonition to a group of women volunteers was: "Ladies, I've never approved of women on the ticket and this is the first time I've permitted a woman to become a candidate. I want to tell you that if you don't turn out as big a vote for her as for a man, there'll never be another woman on the ticket."[34]

As late as 1970, the quaint and yet deep-rooted prejudices not uncommon to political kingmakers were given quite spectacular voicing by none other than a liberal member of the Democratic party's Committee on National Priorities. His remarks came in response to a request by Democratic Congresswoman Patsy Mink of Hawaii for her party to "give the cause of women's rights the highest priority it deserves." Dr. Edgar F. Berman, a close personal friend of former Vice-President Hubert Humphrey, turned a cold shoulder to her appeal, claiming that women were subject to raging hormonal differences which disqualified them for high public office. Said Dr. Berman: "Suppose we had a President in the White House, a menopausal woman President who had to make the decision of the Bay of Pigs. All things being equal, I would still have had a male JFK make the Cuban missile crisis decisions than a female of similar age who could possibly be subject to the curious mental aberrations of that age group."[35]

Dr. Berman's flat disclaimer of women's ability to govern was, naturally, not allowed to stand unchallenged in a period of feminist ferment. Representative Mink, in a widely publicized letter, urged Vice-President Humphrey to seek Dr. Berman's resignation. "I am certain you will be appalled," she said "at Dr. Berman's disgusting performance in which he displayed the basest kind of prejudice against women, characterizing us as mentally incapable to govern,

[33]Quoted in Lawson, p. xxiii.
[34]Quoted in Shalett, "Is There a Women's Vote?" p. 80.
[35]*San Francisco Chronicle,* July 31, 1970, p. 17.

let alone aspire to equality, because we are physiologically inferior." The aftermath to this interesting contretemps was to offer further revelations of the status of women in American politics. Humphrey's response to Mink's challenge to get the "medieval" Dr. Berman to resign was simply to tell her it was a matter between the two. One can well imagine what would have been the outrage on the part of this most liberal champion of causes had it been a different minority so blatantly maligned by a close political associate.

Incredibly, Dr. Berman himself denied harboring any prejudice against women, pointing to his support of liberal policies in the past. Only after the National Organization of Women and prominent feminists got into the fray and public exposure of Dr. Berman's views threatened to embarrass the party was he asked to resign by male comembers of the Democratic National Committee.[36]

To sum up, neither the turnout at the polls nor the involvement and effort in party activities by American women can be blamed for their conspicuous lack of representation in elective offices at all levels of government. Clearly, it is prejudice that stands in their way, prejudice among male power wielders in the parties, for one thing, and possibly also inhibitions and self-denigration among women political activists themselves. The latter is a problem of formidable dimensions and profound implications for the quality of political life, and can best be explored in the context of political socialization. It is ultimately the lack of political consciousness and group cohesion among the most members of this vast "under class" which must be changed if women are to gain the opportunities and advantages sought by the feminists. Yet the important point to be made here is that women's input into the political process entitles them even now to a far greater share of the decision-making positions in the system and to a much greater portion of the politically allocated goods and benefits of the society as well.

Women representatives of the Ninety-first Congress have offered telling testimonies of the difficulties they encountered in running for office. "Even when a woman demonstrates a strong base of support," says Margaret Heckler (R., Mass.), "usually the

---

[36]*San Francisco Chronicle,* July 31, 1970, p. 17.

party hierarchy is the last to see your potential as a candidate."[37] Patsy Mink points to the shortage of campaign funds for women candidates. It is, she says, "partially the result of not being taken seriously by politicians." Although they will go all out to raise funds for the campaign of a rising young man, "they will not do this for a woman." Representative Catherine May (R., Wash.) points out that the new accent on youthful vitality begun in the Kennedy years also puts women at a disadvantage. Family responsibilities usually keep women from entering politics until late in life.

One of the strongest statements came from Shirley Chisholm, black congresswoman from New York: "When I decided to run for Congress, I knew I would encounter both antiblack and anti-feminist sentiments. What surprised me was the much greater virulence of the sex discrimination. ... I was constantly bombarded by both men and women that I should return to teaching, a woman's vocation, and leave politics to men."

Representative Julia Butler Hansen (D., Wash.) finally put the problem in its proper social context: "Every essence of a woman's life prevents her involvement in politics." Quite simply, "the problem is related to the larger question of a woman's role in society."

And so it would seem. We shall take up that question after examining the presumed power of women in other spheres of America's social life.

[37]This and the remarks of the following four women are cited from the *Congressional Quarterly*, Weekly Reports, July 10, 1970, p. 1746.

five

Power's Other Faces

One of the characteristics of myths is that they don't die easily. They persist, in fact, against evidence and in contradiction to the rules of logic and are cherished not for their rational content, but for the comforting or alluring explanations of reality that they offer.

So it is with the myth of woman's power in our society. It is clung to by a great many with little or no basis in reality to support it and it is so hotly defended as to suggest an elaborate system of defense mechanisms in operation. The overbearing woman and the downtrodden male are fantasy figures dear to the hearts of many Americans, as witnessed by the incessant use of these themes in the communications media. Whether these figures are treated in a comic vein or seriously attacked, no cognizance is taken of actual power relations in American society. The male comes out the victim, whether as the dear, trusting clod of a henpecked husband or as the viciously manipulated and "castrated" son of the symbolic Jewish mother. And woman, shame be to her, incessantly conspires to take over, to get or keep the reins of power in her mysteriously strong little hands. Charming she may be while she is at it, but devious, always devious; vile, even, in the vituperative attacks of a Philip Wylie, an Edward Albee, or a Philip Roth. Lacking other devices to interest the public in her "powers," television writers and producers will go to such lengths as to cast her in the role of a witch or genie—in a modern-day setting, yet. The great popularity of the television programs "Bewitched" and "I Dream of Jeanie" in recent years may offer testimony, if not to outright superstitions, at least to the persistent preference among a section of the American public for the myth of woman's supernatural powers. After all—how many *male* witches or genies have we seen on TV lately?

Like all other social phenomena, myths serve certain functions. To discover what these are we have to have a very clear view of the social reality portrayed by a myth and then extrapolate what interests and needs are served by its maintenance. Our examination of both the job market and the political arena indicates very strongly that the particular myth of the power of women in America turns reality on its very head. We must admit, however, that there are other faces of power to be examined. In a pluralist democracy like America, authoritative power—that is, the enforceable right to command others—resides primarily in governmental institutions; but influence—that is, the ability to manipulate the social situation of others or their perception of it—is a special type of power that is distributed in a more complex and elusive manner.[1]

It is, of course, institutionalized power that we are interested in. The power or influence one person may have over another in an intimate relationship is not a very fruitful subject for social analysis. Let it merely be said here that if there were any truth to the supposition that in such situations it is women who are in command or women who can manipulate the actions or perceptions of men, it would stand to reason that this advantage would be used to gain for women benefits and opportunities in other social situations. The whole sorry history of the suppression of women—in all realms of life, up to and including our time—makes a mockery out of the vulgar theory of woman's "bedroom power." The influence a woman may have in a relationship of intimacy with a man may be used to ameliorate her personal situation, but *not* to change her social one.

In examining institutional power we must, moreover, make a distinction between power of position and power of property. The former belongs to the incumbent of any social role or organiza-

---

[1] The definitions offered here are from Gerhard E. Lenski, *Power and Privilege* (New York: McGraw-Hill, 1966), p. 7.

tional office endowed with rightful authority or influence. It is a temporary power, in the sense that persons in possession of it will lose it when they vacate the positions to which it attains. The power incumbent upon owners of great wealth or property does not depend upon incumbency in any office or role—it can be and often is dissociated from it. Wealth and property can, however, be put to use in a variety of ways for the purpose of manipulating the social situation of others or their perception thereof. To mention but a few: Contributions to political campaigns can make or break candidates or force certain issues upon the attention of the public and make for ignoble neglect of other topics, thereby affecting policy outcomes that may have a profound impact upon the daily existence of most of us. Controlling ownership of business properties can be used in such a manner that it changes the very quality of life in a community; decisions of where to locate and when to vacate affect not only the livelihoods of people, but also traffic patterns, pollution, and the tax base of the locality. Wealth can also be parlayed into formidable power when channeled into advertising and full or partial control of the media. The influence these institutions have on our perceptions of social reality is obviously very strong indeed. Wealth can also be used to set up or support tax-exempt foundations or endowments to universities, thereby influencing the direction and use of research in the academic community.

The question of where power resides in America is as complex as it is controversial, but there should be no need, in this instance, to reopen that particular hornet's nest.[2] It is clear from the foregoing analysis that we see the possession of wealth and property as a *power resource* rather than as actual power. What we are trying to do in this part of our study is to identify which institutions in American society exercise control or dominant influence over social situations and the way we perceive them, and then to find what is the role or place of women on the decision-making level of these institutions. We are not concerned, therefore, with the "idle rich," but with the *governing elites,* the persons directly involved with and to varying

---

[2]Interested readers are referred to Robert Dahl, *Who Governs* (New Haven: Yale University Press, 1961); Peter Bachrach and Morton S. Maratz, "The Two Faces of Power," *American Political Science Review* 56 (1962); 947–52; C. Wright Mills, *The Power Elite* (New York: Oxford University Press, 1959); and G. William Domhoff, *Who Rules America?* (Englewood Cliffs, N.J.: Prentice-Hall, 1967).

degrees responsible for the operation of the corporate economy, the shaping of the American polity, and the formation of the educational process.

The central importance of governmental institutions to the whole network of social relationships has already been pointed out. Our examination of women's share of power in this area showed that it was practically nil; the representation of women on all levels of government is disastrously short of even the most flexible notions of what is fair and proper and cannot, therefore, be interpreted as anything but a power vacuum in regard to women. What remains to be seen is whether the absence of women on decision-making levels in politics is repeated in other centers of power in our national life. Where, if anywhere, is the much-reputed power of women to be found?

The Business Elites

We shall start with the corporate economy. Here we are greatly aided in our task by finding general acceptance for the hypothesis that effective control is in the hands of a relatively small number of very large corporations, banks, and insurance companies. As G. William Domhoff points out, there are "awesome statistics buttressing this statement." The nature of control in these large businesses does not present us with much of a problem either, thanks to the summation and impressive analysis presented by Domhoff in his *Who Rules America?* Most authorities, he affirms, find control in the hands of the boards of directors, a relatively small group of individuals who meet regularly to decide upon major company policies. Minor decisions and technical research can be delegated, it is true, but investment policies, for example, and the selection of management are decided by the board. Stockholders do not, by and large, interfere, and extremely few of them have the kind of holdings that might make for any influence in these situations.[3] In 1953, Robert Lampman found that 1 percent of the population held 28.5 percent of the wealth in the United States, and within that 1 percent a much smaller percentage had the bulk of these holdings.[4] Analyz-

---

[3]Domhoff, *Who Rules America?* p. 38.

[4]Roger Lampman, *The Share of Top Wealth Holders in National Wealth, 1956* (Princeton: Princeton University Press, 1962), p. 202.

ing these and other figures offered by prominent economists, Domhoff reaches a conclusion similar to that drawn by C. Wright Mills in *The Power Elite:* "At the very most, 0.2 or 0.3 percent of the adult population own the bulk, the payoff shares, of the corporate world."[5] More often than not it is such substantial shareholdings that give access to corporate directorships.

In his examination of this corporate elite, Domhoff suggests that one can learn enough about this group by focusing in on the top twenty industrials, the top fifteen banks, and the top fifteen insurance companies. What he sought to examine was the social class of the incumbents, while we are interested in their sex. His method makes sense, however, and—like him—we can make a very long story short by pointing out that all of the 884 individuals in question were men. Not one woman was among them.[6] Some minor improvement has, however, taken place recently. My separate study of the top fifteen insurance companies in 1969 found all of eight women among the 201 men on their boards of directors.[7]

Looking at *all* large banks and corporations, Dr. Margaret Cussler confirms that only a handful of women are on the boards of directors of these institutions.[8] In 1956, *Fortune* magazine estimated that of the about 250,000 "real" executives in the country, a mere 5,000—2 percent—were women.[9] It is a fair bet that these are still in the middle-management positions, rather than on the highest levels. As of 1969, women in retailing, the most traditional female executive stronghold, occupied but an "infinitesimal" number of first-rank executive positions, according to William Burston of the National Retail Merchants Association.[10] The same year found 270 women among 14,172 bank chairmen or presidents, but it is indicated that the majority of this lucky 2 percent presided over small family banks and owed their positions to inheritance.[11] A *Business Week* survey of women in business at this

[5]Quoted in Domhoff, *Who Rules America?* p. 45.

[6]Domhoff, p. 51.

[7]The fifteen companies and information about their directors are taken from *Moody's Insurance and Financial Stocks: Monthly Reference List,* December 8, 1969.

[8]Margaret Cussler, *The Woman Executive* (New York: Harcourt, Brace & World, 1958).

[9]This figure is equivalent to approximately 2 percent of the total number of "real" executives in this country at that time.

[10]*Business Week,* August 2, 1969, p. 44.

[11]*Business Week,* August 2, 1969, p. 44.

time (1969) found that American industry produced as few top women executives as it had ten years earlier.[12]

Whether one chooses to emphasize directors or high-level executives as the important power wielders in the corporate economy, it is clear that women are just not cut in. To be really thorough, we might also examine how many women are to be found among corporation lawyers, since these are known to be closely linked to the business elite and to have an influence that "goes far beyond the giving of advice on legal matters."[13] Both C. Wright Mills and A. A. Berle, analysts of widely different political views, point to the central role played by the corporation lawyer. Mills finds him performing the function of the "go-between" effectively and powerfully; transcending "the narrow world of any one industry," he is "in a position to speak and act for the corporate world or at least sizeable portions of it. The corporation lawyer," concludes Mills, "is a key link between the economic and military and political areas."[14] Berle affirms that corporation law firms "become virtually an annex to some groups of financial promoters, manipulators, or industrialists." Not only do they dominate the legal profession, but "what they have contributed . . . is the creation of a legal framework for the new economic system, built largely around the modern corporation."[15]

We gain a very good insight into women's role in the power-invested world of corporation law from an authoritative study by Erwin O. Smiegel.[16] First, it should be pointed out that the influential law firms are usually very large and that most of them are situated in New York City or have branches there. Of the 1,755 women attorneys in New York, Erwin found only 18 listing themselves as working in large offices. In the New York City branches of the large firms with headquarters elsewhere, only one woman law partner could be found. Women, it turned out, were usually not even given a chance to enter corporation law. Of the lawyers who wished to engage a law clerk, considered to be the springboard to a

[12]*Business Week,* August 2, 1969, p. 42.

[13]Robert A. Gordon, quoted in Domhoff, *Who Rules America?,* p. 59.

[14]Mills, *The Power Elite,* p. 289.

[15]A. A. Berle, Jr., *Encyclopedia of the Social Sciences* (New York: Macmillan, 1948), 9:341.

[16]Erwin O. Smiegel, *The Wall Street Lawyer* (New York: Free Press, 1964).

career in this field, 90 percent refused to even interview women lawyers for the job. Interviews of the few female associates found revealed that they felt they had little chance to advance to partnership. Large law firms, they pointed out, were too much like male clubs—women were simply not wanted.

The Very Rich

The absence of women among the governing elite in the corporate economy is the more conspicuous for the fact that women do account for about *one-third* of the top wealth holders in this country.[17] Also, in recent years women have accounted for slightly more than 48 percent of the adult shareholding population. The number of shares owned individually by women stockholders equaled 18 percent of the total as compared with 24 percent owned individually by men. The remaining 58 percent were held by institutions, brokers and dealers, persons with joint accounts, nominees, and foreign owners.[18] Although these figures already belie the assertion that women own most of the wealth in the country, their share of it certainly seems to be large enough for at least the small minority of wealthy women to gain access to decision-making positions in the corporate economy. So what has happened here?

Apart from the customary prejudices and inhibitions operating in this as in all other institutional settings, it must be pointed out that women's control over their share of wealth in America is subject to a number of qualifications. First, they come into it at an older age than men. More than one-third of the women wealth holders examined by Lampman are widows over sixty years of age, and most of them inherited their holdings from a deceased husband. Of the remaining women among the top wealth holders, about three-quarters are married and they are usually the beneficiaries of bequests and transfers set up by their husbands or fathers to take advantage of loopholes in tax legislation.[19] More than twice as

[17] Lampman, *The Share of Top Wealth Holders*, p. 100. Also confirmed in a study by the Internal Revenue Service, 1972.

[18] U.S. Department of Labor, Women's Bureau, *The 1969 Handbook on Women Workers* (Washington, D.C.: Government Printing Office, 1969) pp. 145–46.

[19] Sylvia Porter, "Did Women Cause Panic Black Monday?" *Sacramento Bee*, June 18, 1962, p. 11.

many women as men, affirms Sylvia Porter, obtain their first share of stock through inheritance or as a gift.[20] Also, more women than men are the beneficiaries of estates left in trust.

The implications of these findings are quite clear: women wealth holders are not likely to have the expertise, the experience, or the opportunity for putting their resources to use in an attempt to influence the trend and shape of the economy. This conclusion is affirmed by several of the top financiers of the country. Veteran Wall Streeter Gerald M. Loeb points out that stock ownership by women does not mean that they handle their own financial business. "As a matter of fact," he says, "I rarely see a woman handling her own account—it's usually a banker, a broker, her attorney, or a relative, *but it's a man.*"[21] Albert E. Schwabacher, Jr., a San Francisco investment banker, also discounts the theory that women are about to take over the economy. They may own about half of the *personal* property in the United States and perhaps a smaller percentage of the real estate, but much of it is handled by professional managers and brokers. "My own guess is," says Schwabacher, "that they actually control not more than 15 to 20 percent of our total national wealth. Obviously, this constitutes neither a national emergency nor a national opportunity."[22] A vice-president of the brokerage firm of Merrill Lynch, Pierce, Fenner & Smith affirms that women are not nearly as important in trading as people think—only one out of every five of their stock customers is a woman. In 1962, for example, women accounted for only 25.5 percent of all trading on the New York Stock Exchange.[23] At the same time, it must be remembered that only a tiny minority *within* the minority of women stockholders have the amount of shares necessary to make their influence felt in the management and operations of major corporations.[24] That, together with the other factors limiting women's effective use of their wealth holdings, makes all of the noise and furor about women's takeover of the economy nothing but ludicrous.

[20]Porter, p. 11.
[21]Lampman, *The Share of Top Wealth Holders,* p. 241.
[22]*Sacramento Union,* November 22, 1955, p. 9
[23]Sylvia Porter, "Did Women Cause Panic?," p. 11.
[24]Robert Lampman reports 253,000 women with gross estates of $60,000 or more in 1953. Lampman, *The Share of Top Wealth Holders,* p. 191.

The Labor Oligarchy

There is one more institution to consider as we examine the exercise of power in the corporate economy. Organized labor has, in the past few decades, established itself fairly securely as a group with influence and something close to a veto, if not affirmative decision-making power, in the economic and political system. The governing elites in the corporate system are clearly somewhat restricted in their exercise of control by the activities of labor, on the levels both of bargaining and of political action. As an interest group, labor constitutes one of the most formidable elements in what Schattschneider has called "the pressure system"[25]—the conglomerate of interest groups and private associations that are supposed to serve as the link between the individual citizen and the government. *How much* weight can be assigned to labor in the operation of the pressure system is still a matter of controversy; but even though "the flaw in the pluralist's heaven," in Schattschneider's caustic words, "is that the angels sing with an upper-class accent,"[26] labor must be conceded the ability to halt or to restrain, if not always to block, corporate acts not to their liking.

Women do have a place in the labor movement, as we know. With nearly 40 percent of the working force being women, they very well should. Although they are not to be found in unions with the ratio we would expect, given their participation in the labor market, there were still 5.3 million women union members in 1972. One out of every seven women workers belongs to a union, compared to one out of every four men workers. Also in 1974, 88 percent of women members belonged to the AFL-CIO and the remaining 12 percent to unaffiliated unions.[27] Among union members in 1966, one out of every five was a woman.

We should expect, therefore, that at least in this sector of our social life women have gained a significant share of decision-making power and a chance to influence the shape and direction of the corporate economy. Like most other organizations, however,

[25] E. E. Schattschneider, *The Semi-Sovereign People* (New York: Holt, Rinehart and Winston, 1969).

[26] Schattschneider, *The Semi-Sovereign People.*

[27] Virginia A. Bergquist, "Women's Participation in Labor Organizations," *Monthly Labor Review,* October 1974, pp. 3–9.

the AFL-CIO is effectively controlled by an oligarchy of leaders. The executive council of the AFL-CIO is most important in the hierarchy, but local leadership also exerts authority over union members, as well as representing them in negotiations with employers. Union hierarchies have, in a sense, "edged into the process of industrial administration," according to V.O. Key, "and have a hand, through bargaining, in the formulation of policy on promotions, transfers, layoffs, fringe benefits, methods of production, and other such matters. If we regard the process of governing as the imposition of rules of behavior, unions in reality govern as well as agitate."[28]

For us the question becomes then: have women made it into the union hierarchies? The answer in both earlier and recent studies is very clearly negative: women have remained rare at the governing and high appointive levels of almost all of the 177 nationwide unions in the United States, as Virginia A. Bergquist points out. Despite the progress in female union membership, the number of women in the highest national union offices increased only slightly during the last ten years.[29]

How bad it is will be revealed by the following data: In unions with at least 50,000 women members, only 6 were among the 187 selected national officers and appointed officials in 1972.[30] On the executive boards of these unions, only 18 women were included among the 556 members.

The AFL-CIO, where women account for an estimated 25 percent of the union membership, provides a dramatic illustration of women's lack of decision-making power in the union movement. No women are included in the 35-member Executive Council of the organization; moreover, in the state labor councils, only 8 women were found among the 173 officers and officials in 1972.[31]

The fall 1975 national convention of the AFL-CIO held in San Francisco provided further glimpses into the overwhelming male

---

[28]V.O. Key, Jr., *Politics, Parties, and Pressure Groups,* 4th ed. (New York: Crowell, 1961), p. 65.

[29]Bergquist, "Women's Participation in Labor Organizations," p. 4. See also K. Amundsen, *The Silenced Majority* (Englewood Cliffs, N.J.: Prentice-Hall, Inc., 1971), p. 97.

[30]Bergquist, p. 7

[31]Bergquist, p. 8.

domination here. Of the 872 delegates, a mere 22 were women. Predictably, demands from the female delegates for a separate women's department or election of a woman to the all-male Executive Council were buried without protest.[32]

The situation was neatly summed up by Aileen Hernandez, former president of the National Organization for Women, in an address to the Industrial Relations Research Association in the fall of 1974: America's unions, she said, are all run by "antiquated white middleclass men whose minds are back in the 1900s."[33] The consequences, for women, are formidable, indeed. As Ms. Hernandez pointed out, contract proposals for maternity leave and child-care centers are the ones the unions drop first. The negotiation teams are simply not made up of women.

The static nature of the labor union movement has been deplored by nearly all activists in recent years. According to Ms. Hernandez: "If trade unions are ever to become viable again, they are going to have to reach out from this narrow pool and address all the working people in the society, which means women, too."

This is precisely one of the major aims of a promising new organization within the movement, the Coalition of Labor Union Women (CLUW). Convened in Chicago in March 1974 with 3,200 delegates from fifty-eight labor unions, the objectives agreed on included fighting sexism within the unions as well as in society, and, most importantly, placing a greater emphasis on organizing unorganized women.

Myra Wolfgang, a vice-president of the Hotel and Restaurant Employees Union from Detroit, expressed the prevailing sentiment among CLUW members at the 1975 AFL-CIO convention:

> The foot that is in the door is not encased in a ballet slipper hiding twinkletoes. It is a marching shoe that intends to march jointly with the men of the labor movement to address itself to the problems of millions of unorganized women of this country.[34]

To sum up: the U.S. corporate economy even as late as the

[32]*San Francisco Chronicle,* October 6, 1975, p. 5.
[33]*San Francisco Chronicle,* November 18, 1974.
[34]Quoted in the *San Francisco Chronicle,* October 5, 1975, p. 14.

mid-seventies is still run, managed, and/or controlled with precious little involvement of women on the key decision-making levels. The female half of the nation has virtually no representation among either the governing business elites or the hierarchy in the labor unions. That women are important as consumers is obvious enough, but this "countervailing power" is hardly more than a fond memory or a distant hope in this age of high-pressure advertising, oligopolistic structures and price fixing. Unless women become a truly formidable pressure group in the political arena, the power void confronting them in this additional important sphere of our national life is very serious indeed.

Mass Media

Power in the mass media is power to be reckoned with in modern society, for the messages transmitted through newspapers, radio, television, and magazines have considerable influence on our perception of social reality in general and on our political orientations in particular. We no longer have a society of publics, where there is frequent interaction between people on the intellectual and political levels where people formulate different viewpoints on the basis of this interaction, organize around them, and compete for their viewpoint to win out in the arena of politics. In a mass society, as C. Wright Mills points out (and we have moved a considerable distance toward it), the dominant type of communication consists of the formal media; publics become mere markets for these media. The ebb and flow of discussion must still be considered, and informal opinion leaders can be important in changing perceptions and attitudes; but then, *their* messages, too, are by and large transmitted through the media.[35]

This is not to suggest that we are confronted with an all-powerful, monolithic force set to brainwash and manipulate the American people. The media convey to us different images, con-

[35]For an examination of the role of opinion leaders in the context of a media-dominated society, see Elihu Katz, "The Two-step Flow of Communications: An Up-to-date Report on an Hypothesis," *Public Opinion Quarterly* 21 (1957) 61–78, and C. Wright Mills, "Mass Media and Public Opinion," in I. L. Horowitz, ed., *Power, Politics, and People: The Collected Essays of C. Wright Mills* (New York: Ballantine Books, 1963), pp. 577–99.

flicting messages, and varying interpretations that afford and encourage clashes of opinions among individuals and, on the whole,
scholars in the field have found effective mass communication to
function more frequently as an agent of reinforcement than as an
agent of change.[36] Yet the media are crucial in carrying through
political messages today. Access to and effective use of television,
for instance, can build up candidates and focus attention upon
issues that would otherwise be destined to obscurity. The meteoric
rise in politics of former Governor Ronald Reagan of California,
for example, and the against-all-odds success of Cesar Chavez's
drive to organize farmworkers, could not conceivably have come
about without television's spotlights. Reagan, before 1966, was a
likable, but not too prominent, actor whose political aspirations
occasioned surprise or chuckles among most Californians; then he
captivated TV audiences with his highly polished deliveries of messages dear to their hearts. And Chavez was a missionary without
money, influence, or the power of a large following; then the plight
of farmworkers and his fight on their behalf was dramatized by
TV, bringing liberal and radical sympathizers flocking to his cause.
Power to affect the political orientations of people is perhaps the
most crucial form of power in a democracy; as already suggested, it
is only through politics that institutional arrangements and resource distribution can be effectively and seriously challenged.

How do women stand, then, in regard to this important resource
in American society? What is their representation among decision
makers in the media, that is, among the groups and individuals
with authority to fire and hire communicators, to accept and reject
programs and messages, and to initiate new approaches and test
them in the field? Also, how do women figure among the communicators themselves? What inroads have they made in the areas
of writing, interpreting, editing, and producing for any and all of
the media? Here should be a very important measure of the
influence of women on the perceptions held of themselves by both
sexes. Here is also to be found a good measure of their part in
shaping the American polity, as G. William Domhoff terms it.

The major networks must be attended to first. On the board of
ABC, there was not one woman among the fifteen directors in

---

[36]These findings are effectively summarized in Richard E. Dawson and Kenneth
Prewitt, *Political Socialization* (Boston: Little, Brown, 1969).

1970. At NBC, one woman director found her way in among fifteen males. In surveying presidents, vice-presidents, and general managers of television stations throughout the country, there were *no* women in this influential group in all of *thirty-seven* states.

The picture is somewhat better at the level of individual stations, though any survey of TV reportage and stories will confirm the conclusion drawn in a number of studies to date: men dominate markedly, both in terms of hosts, news reporters, and stars of individual shows and series.[37] A survey of high-level TV station employees in 1972 yielded the results in Table 5.1.

TABLE 5.1   Employees of 609 TV Stations, 1972

	Officials and Managers		Professional Employees	
	Female	*Male*	*Female*	*Male*
White	477	4,773	843	6,306
Black	23	77	119	386
Oriental	12	14	8	35
American Indian	3	9	5	16
Spanish American	15	112	35	172

Source: Media Report to Women (Washington, D.C., 1973).

The "sexual wasteland," as television is sometimes called, is not much improved upon in terms of male dominance as we look at the major newspapers of the country. Though the *Washington Post* is one of the few such papers with a female publisher, and a very distinguished one at that, a recent study by Dorothy McGhee gives us the following male/female breakdown: managing editors, 10/0; news desk editors, 9/0; finance and other special sections, 9/0; metropolitan, national, and foreign desk editors, 50/3; fashion or style section, 7/1.[38]

What about Affirmative Action? Indications are that more women are now reporting the hard news than before, but this may be due to the influence of women's rights groups and lobbies more than the operation of Affirmative Action plans. A study of United

[37]Helen F. Franzwa, "Women and Television: An Annotated Bibliography." Unpublished paper, April 1975.
[38]*Media Report to Women.*

Press International news service in 1972 revealed that one year's progress under such a plan brought about the addition of *one* woman professional employee.[39]

Higher Education

America's universities, debunked in common parlance as "knowledge factories," have a special relationship to power. By themselves, these institutions do not have the capability to challenge and effect change in present power arrangements; yet by educating scholars and intellectuals they may have a decisive influence on what knowledge is to be transmitted and how it is to be used. Thereby, power structures will be affected, either in the direction of reinforcement or in the direction of rejection. Ideas can be formidable weapons. The intellectual's superior ability either to justify or debunk authority makes him politically relevant—a source of potential trouble as well as necessary sustenance for the governing elites of a democracy, for in our society power has to be legitimized or, at the very least, concealed. Its possessors have to have earned their positions, according to our most basic beliefs. The consent of the governed must be obtained—or their indifference to the arrangement insured. And it is when these subtle and yet explosive political questions come up that intellectuals figure prominently on the scene. The main reason for the mounting attacks on universities in the late sixties may very well be the increasing and well-publicized unwillingness on the part of their incumbents to accept and cooperate with the status quo. The massive research coming out of the top universities must be kept flowing to its places of destination, be it corporations, agribusiness, or government. In the status quo perspective, students and their professors must be kept in line to the point, at least, where they do not interfere with that flow or succeed in arousing significant portions of the public to challenge present power structures.

As both faculties and students have sadly come to realize, it is the boards of trustees or boards of regents of the universities that have the real power in this sphere. Faculties, no matter how well organized, have found themselves undercut and overlooked on so many occasions that it is clear that their "autonomy" is subject to the

[39] *Media Report to Women.*

tolerance and will of other power wielders. College presidents hold some sway still and can, with superior tactical skill, go a long way toward making the boards accept policies and proposals considered essential by faculty and students. But college presidents, too, can be replaced—even summarily dismissed. So it is to the boards we must look for the kind of power that can shape and direct higher education and its uses in America. And it is to the elite universities and the largest state universities we must look to find the institutions that influence and set the standards for the whole educational apparatus. Again, one must keep in mind the central importance of government to these operations—not just the state universities, but also the private ones depend on governmental subsidiaries and/or research grants today. But we already know the answer to our question about government; what we are after now is the share of power accorded women in the governing of higher education. And that, at this point, means primarily women's share of positions on the boards of trustees of the top universities. To a lesser, but significant extent, it also means women's representation on the boards of foundations giving substantial grants to universities.

We shall start with the boards of trustees.[40] In our examination of twenty-one major U.S. institutions of higher learning in 1969, we found that in five there were no women on the boards of trustees. The Universities of Kansas, Illinois, and Colorado, plus Yale and Harvard, had not one woman representative among the 45 trustees on their respective governing boards. In the remaining sixteen institutions, there were 34 women among 492 men. That amounts to less than a 7 percent representation for the 51 percent majority of this country in this additional important sphere of America's institutional life. The institutions examined were, in addition to the five mentioned above: the Universities of Georgia, Southern California, California, Iowa, Maryland, Minnesota, Wisconsin, Virginia, State University of New York, and Pittsburgh, Reed College, and Stanford, Duke, and George Washington Universities. Needless to say, none of these has a woman president.

The publicly supported system of higher education in California, considered a model for other states in most respects, offers an instructive example of the place and status accorded women in the

---

[40]Our data are derived from examination of 1969 college catalogues of the respective universities.

governance of such enterprises. In the more than one hundred years since the creation of the University of California (its "birth-date" is 1867), only three women have sat on its Board of Regents. One, no longer serving, succeeded her husband upon his death. In the state university system, only two women sat on the Board of Trustees in the mid-seventies.

In other associations and committees considered important in shaping the cultural-intellectual climate of this country, women are equally noted for their absence. It takes but the briefest look to note the nearly exclusive male makeup of the four organizations in this area considered key ones by G. William Domhoff in his *Who Rules America?*:[41] the Council on Foreign Relations, the Foreign Policy Association, the Committee for Economic Development, and the National Advertising Council. If we pay attention also to the extensive and partially covert public relations programs of the CIA, the FBI, and the various branches of our military, it is equally obvious that, again, women have little or no say.

We started this examination by suggesting that to discover the function of a myth we have to explore the social reality portrayed by it, for myths serve to conceal, to soften, and to rationalize our actual social relationships—to make them more bearable, as it were, both for those on the outs and for those favored in any common situation. Particularly when the reality is rather hard to bear, when the power relationships conflict with cherished principles of justice and fairness, when the victimization of fellow humans is too obvious and crude, myths are fostered and take hold among people. One might say, then, that myths serve us all well—except that as they obscure reality, they get in the way of needed change.

The myth of woman's power in America does just that. It does, indeed, turn reality on its very head and thereby serves to imprison both men and women in a fuzzy, alluring fantasy that tends to immobilize anyone who wants to change the present power relationships. As long as the myth persists, as long as we continue to be blinded, women will have no more of their share of power than they do now. In the centers of power in our national life, what that amounts to is virtually *nothing*.

[41]Domhoff, *Who Rules America?*, p. 64.

six

The Ideology of Sexism

Are women persons? The question was raised, tongue in cheek, by Adrienne Koch at a symposium on "Man and Civilization" arranged by the University of California a few years ago. Considering the pervasive and serious discrimination against women in every important sphere of America's social and political life, such an inquiry, it seems to us, ought to be taken quite seriously. In a society where the dominant creed calls for freedom, justice, and equality of opportunity for all, the existence of grave inequities and systematic subordination of a major group in the population can only be rationalized on the basis of a common belief that members of this group are somehow different, somehow outside the norm set for full-fledged citizens, somehow not quite equal. A degree of inferiority must be assumed in regard to women for members of both sexes to accept so willingly and unquestioningly the relegation of the feminine majority to a secondary status and a subordinate rank in every stratum they have found their way into. Male domination has to be considered *normal* and woman's inferior assignation *proper* for the sexist institutions to function as smoothly as they do.

Such was the problem with blacks in American society at the time that Gunnar Myrdal took up his investigation of *An American Dilemma*.[1] It was a problem, said Myrdal, in the hearts of white

[1] Gunnar Myrdal, *An American Dilemma* (New York: Harper & Brothers, 1944).

Americans—having in theory committed themselves to the "American creed," with the postulates described above, they could live with the institution of racism only by assuming the inherent inferiority of black Americans or by determinedly ignoring the existence of this national shame. For this situation to change, it was first of all necessary for black citizens to force the problem upon the attention of the American public, to confront their white countrymen with demands to end this intolerable injustice, and to make it impossible to evade and ignore this festering sore within the body politic. Then, and only then, could the problem be properly attacked and the practices and structures of racism be eradicated from American life.

Again, the parallel with the problems of women is striking. One important question left unattended by Myrdal was, however, how the members of a group suppressed so gravely for so long were to overcome the feelings of inferiority and the habits of deference inculcated in them throughout their lifetime; for one of the most debilitating effects of racial prejudice, as Kenneth Clark has shown, is that the victims come to believe in and even cherish their "inferiority."[2] The "Uncle Tom" mentality had to be changed before victims of racism could start on their move. No easy task, that, given the fact that the whole socialization process was geared to make blacks believe in and accept their inferior roles.

It can, as we now know, be done. But it is crucial to understand that suppression of women, like that of blacks, rests ultimately on what is believed about their innate nature and their proper and necessary role in society. This sets the context in which decisions are made for and against giving access to and allowing the advance of women in any one field of activity and in which behavior is judged as either appropriate or inappropriate. Just as important, women's self-concepts are to a very great extent dependent on the core of imputed and preferred feminine attributes prevailing in the society. Rationalizations for discrimination against women are provided by just this set of interrelated beliefs and values in regard to woman's real nature and proper place. What I am talking about here is an ideology—the ideology, I will suggest, of sexism. Its

---

[2]Quoted in M. Homer, "Woman's Will to Fail," *Psychology Today*, November 1969, p. 36.

beliefs and postulates are well integrated, its functions to direct and guide social and political activity, and it rests on assumptions that are not reliably tested, but that to some degree are accepted on faith.[3]

The "Natural" Woman

What are the components of this ideology? They are easily discovered, actually—familiar to all of us, accepted without question by many, and challenged by only a few. Its first tenets are that woman is different from man, in psychological as well as biological makeup, and that she consequently has a different role to play in the human environment. The "true" nature of woman has been depicted—ad nauseam—not just in mass media and popular literature, but also by a seemingly endless line of psychologists, sociologists, and anthropologists eager to add their voices to the choir of sexist conformity. The basic idea is that for women— although no longer for other human groups, oddly enough—*biology is destiny.* The mere facts that she bears children and has menstrual periods make her the prey to hormonal influences that shape her temperament and abilities in certain distinct ways. Woman is supposed to be more emotional than man, less able to apply logic to problems and situations, more conforming, and less aggressive, but also more devious and superior, naturally, in possession of that mysterious "feminine" quality, intuition.

In its most benevolent forms, sexist ideology becomes paternalistic in its protective approach and fawning tone. Take, for example, this description of feminine "nature" offered by a highly praised and well-read marriage counselor, G. O. Payetter:

> Feelings, moods and attitudes . . . rule a woman, not facts, reason nor logic.
> By herself, woman is all mixed up, but superb as an auxiliary. . . .
> A woman is inanimate or on the defensive until you create a feeling such as praise. Then she goes all out.

[3]This is the definition of an ideology offered, for example, by William E. Connolly, *Political Science and Ideology* (New York: Atherton Press, 1967). For a more thorough discussion of the concept, see Karl Mannheim, *Ideology and Utopia* (New York: Harcourt, Brace & World, 1936), pp. 55–109.

Never scold or explain when she is angry, remember she is feeling, not thinking. . . .

Stop bossing; just manipulate her in her feelings. . . . The acquisition of knowledge and responsibilities does not lessen woman's need for support, guidance, control. Quite the contrary.

Why ask women when they only need to be told? Why ask women when they hope to be taken?[4]

Feminine virtues are, indeed, extolled in the most extravagant manner by precisely those who insist that woman cannot, because of her nature, aspire to the status and heights of achievement in politics or intellectual or artistic work attained by a man. The charm of women, their gentleness, and their sensitivity to the sufferings of others are invariably held up as qualities special to their sex and, moreover, as qualities so attractive that they more than make up for women's lesser abilities in other areas. The possession of such virtues should presumably be gratifying enough to women to leave them satisfied with a secondary status. Witness, for instance, the self-defense of Dr. Edgar F. Berman of recent "hormonal-rage" fame. Having put Representative Patsy Mink and other women politicians firmly in place by insisting that "there just are psychological and physical inhibitants that limit a woman's potential," he hastened to add: "The same glandular secretions producing the reactions which you say do not exist, endow most 'real women' with their most endearing and genteel charms." And although these splendid characteristics do not make possible any great accomplishment by women, they are "charms which help balance and restrain the aggressive male."[5]

The position goes back to Freud himself, of course, the originator of extravagant speculations about women's "penis envy." The intellectual creator of the defeat-inducing feminine triad —masochism, narcissism, and passivity—also had chivalrous compliments to pay to "the most delightful thing this world can offer us—our ideal of womanhood." Nature, he suggests, "has determined woman's destiny through beauty, charm, and sweetness."[6]

[4]G. O. Payetter, "How to Get and Hold a Woman," quoted in Paula Stern, "The Womanly Image: Character Assassination through the Ages," *Atlantic Monthly,* March 1970, pp. 87–91.

[5]*San Francisco Chronicle,* July 31, 1970, p. 17.

[6]Ernest Jones, *The Life and Work of Sigmund Freud* (New York: Basic Books, 1953), 1:175.

To this imposing father of psychology, his chosen partner for life was, naturally, "my sweet child" or "my precious little woman."[7]

The "nurturant" qualities of woman, cherished so highly by sexist psychologists in their more benevolent moods, are also enthusiastically supported by modern sociologists. The terms change, as we move into another discipline, but the assumptions of biologically based attributes and their ascription remain the same. The female, in Talcott Parsons's analysis, becomes "expressive" and the male "instrumental."[8] This is the leading sociologist of recent decades speaking, and the traits that go with these descriptions complement precisely those proclaimed to be feminine or masculine by psychologists, according to "Parsonian" Orville G. Brim.[9] For a woman to be expressive means, on the positive side, for her to be kind, obedient, cheerful, affectionate, and sensitive. All very well—until we compare these "proper" qualities for woman with their counterparts for the man and speculate on the political implications following from such assignations. For a man to be expressive means to be tenacious, curious, ambitious, responsible, original, and competitive—all qualities required of a governing class. The nonaggressive, highly emotional, submissive, cheerful, and affectionate member of the other sex—the "natural" woman as composed by psychology and sociology—is perfectly suited to take second place. Gunnar Myrdal's description of the situation of the black citizen[10] applies equally as well to that of woman: her assumed graces and her assumed vices fit her very appropriately for the inferior position assigned to her, for with the "nurturant" qualities and charms of woman go her masochism, envy, and narcissism, according to Freud—or her tattling, teasing, jealousy, exhibitionism, negativism, affinity for quarrel, and inability to cooperate, according to Brim.

We all know this "natural" woman. How deeply ingrained her image is in folk culture is easily perceived by surveying popular

---

[7]See Ernest Freud, *Letters of Sigmund Freud* (New York: Harcourt, Brace & World, 1960), p. 161.

[8]Talcott Parsons and R. F. Bales, *Family, Socialization, and Interaction Process* (New York: Free Press, 1955).

[9]Orville G. Brim, Jr., "Family Structure and Sex Role Learning by Children," in Robert Winch, Robert McGinnis, and Herbert Barringer, eds., *Selected Studies in Marriage and the Family* (New York: Holt, Rinehart and Winston, 1962), pp. 286–87.

[10]Myrdal, *An American Dilemma.*

literature, the media, and even children's books. In her analysis of popular magazines and movies in the post-World War II period, Betty Friedan found that almost without exception the "real" woman was depicted as submissive, nonambitious, and totally oriented toward loving and caring for man and children. The woman who escaped this norm, determined to go against her destiny in pursuing a career, was invariably described as frustrated, insecure, and masculinized, and, of course, was doomed to failure or perpetual gloom.[11] Such heart-warming images have also penetrated television, and with a vengeance. The typical woman here —in commercials, dramas, or situation comedies—is unpredictable, emotional, and irrational, but mixes her feminine wiliness with just the proper amount of feminine sweetness to, presumably, still appeal as a model of womanhood. Never, or hardly ever, is she a highly rational or ambitious figure with clear-cut career goals or dedication to something other than marriage, family, or courtship. If she, the poor thing, is found to be working in the man's world of business or professions, it is understood that this is a temporary affair, induced usually by widowhood—preferably *not* by divorce. What she really wants is to stay home, and what she inevitably and perpetually is after is a man. In commercials, she is not only irrational and submissive—even to the strangest male intruders, often in ghost or sheik form—she is also helpless, so helpless that she will gladly follow the advice and direction of not only the weird samples of male superiority but also that of voices—male, naturally —coming out of walls. Susan Brownmiller, journalist and TV news reporter, said it: "The image of women in the commercials is that of *stupidity*." Actress Anselma Del-Olio adds that they picture woman as a "mindless boob or masochistic slave." And Ti-Grace Atkinson, writer and founder of the Feminists, points out what is obvious to many: "Women are shown exclusively as sex objects and reproducers—not as whole people."[12]

It is in children's literature that the put-down of women is started, however, and it is not hard to guess at its influence on the developing, accepting minds of young readers. Elisabeth Fisher, writer and editor, found "an almost incredible conspiracy of condi-

---

[11]Betty Friedan, *The Feminine Mystique* (New York: Dell, 1963).
[12]Quoted in Edith Efron, "Is Television Making a Mockery of the American Woman?" *TV Guide*, August 8–14, 1970, p. 7.

tioning" as she investigated books for young children in stores and libraries.[13] There is, first of all, a serious omission. In the world of picture books, females appear in only about 20 to 30 percent of illustrations. Moreover, when girls appear, they are shown in their relation to boys, and are depicted as passive, though sometimes manipulative. "They walk, read, or dream," Fisher points out. "They seldom ride bicycles; if they do it, it is seated behind a boy as in Dr. Seuss's *One Fish, Two Fish, Red Fish, Blue Fish*. When I came across a little girl sailing paper boats, I was overwhelmed with gratefulness."

Working mothers don't exist in this never-never land of children's picture books. One book in which they do appear is known of, Eve Meriam's *Mommies Who Work*, but Miss Fisher found it out of stock in all the stores she visited. In other books the stereotypes of male activity, female passivity, male involvement with things and women's with emotions, and male dominance and female subordination persist. Comments Elisabeth Fisher:

> Though there have been women doctors in this country for over a hundred years, and pediatrics is one of their preferred specialties, there is not a single woman doctor to be found [in children's books]. Women are nurses, librarians, teachers—but the principal is always male. They have emotions: they get angry; they disagree; they smile; they disapprove or are disapproved of; they want to please. What they do not do, is act. Boys do. Girls are—a highly artificial and unsatisfactory dichotomy.

The offense is repeated in school textbooks, from primary readers on. Marjorie Uren of Stanford University was shocked at the depth and pervasiveness of sex prejudice discovered in a great number of texts researched.[14] Women are either ignored— apparent noncontributors to history, civilization, and culture— or they are pictured in stereotyped roles as appendages or tresses to men. Recently, the new line of textbooks adopted by the State of California for use in primary grades came under special

[13]Elisabeth Fisher, "The Second Sex, Junior Division," *New York Times Book Review*, May 1969, pp. 6–44.

[14]Unpublished research, reported at a hearing of the California Legislature's Education Committee, May 12, 1970.

scrutiny. Virginia Kidd of the Department of Speech and Communication at Sacramento State College found sexual roles dramatized in the following way:

> "Mark! Janet . . .!" said Mother.
> "What is going on here?"
>
> "She cannot skate," said Mark.
> "I can help her.
> I want to help her.
> Look at her, Mother.
> Just look at her.
> She is just like a girl.
> She gives up."
>
> Mother forces Janet to try again.
>
> "Now you see," said Mark.
> "Now you can skate.
> But just with me to help you."[15]

Janet, naturally, doesn't make suggestions of this kind to Mark. Mark's toys are the toys of adventure—a parachute, a rocket, a helmet, and so forth—and Mark aspires to be an astronaut. Janet's toys are all home-bound: a playhouse, dolls, a buggy, dishes. But then, Mother's chief occupation in the readers is also washing dishes, cooking, ironing, sewing—and wearing aprons. Daddy's chief occupation is coming home—and playing ball with Mark.

Such are the images and such is the world that sexist ideology would proscribe for us. The inherent inferiority of the female of the species is subtly suggested and persistently conveyed in media messages, textbooks, literature, and even science. We do not seem to have moved very far from the definition of femininity offered by Aristotle: "A certain lack of qualities; we should regard the female nature as afflicted with natural defectiveness." More than two thousand years later, former Vice-President Agnew had this insight to offer: "Three things have been difficult to tame—the ocean,

---

[15]Virginia Kidd, "Now You See, Said Mark," *New York Review of Books*, September 3, 1970, pp. 35–37.

fools, and women. We may soon be able to tame the ocean; fools and women will take a little longer."[16]

The Sexual Orthodoxy and Its Defenders

It is interesting to note that the psychologists' idea of woman's nature has provided sexist ideology with just the scientific cloak it needs in this age of egalitarian philosophies. On the basis of the "knowledge" that woman is less intellectually assertive, less ambitious, and more emotional than man, that she has less superego and therefore weaker social interests, one can with great ease assign her to traditional roles and to the place to which she was always accustomed—behind the man. The penis envy Freud considered to be a dominant theme in all feminine life "inevitably causes women to feel inferior to men. These deep-seated feelings of inadequacy can be compensated for only partially by giving birth to a male child." Not just any child, mind, it has to be male. And "masochism and passivity . . . are natural aspects of normal femininity." From which follows, according to one of Freud's prominent interpreters, that "whenever a woman behaves in a nonpassive or aggressive way or competes with men, she is being neurotically unfeminine."[17]

What this all means in practical terms is spelled out with seeming satisfaction by other prominent psychologists. As late as 1965, Bruno Bettelheim of the University of Chicago could tell us that "we must start with the realization that as much as women want to be good scientists or engineers, they want first and foremost to be womanly companions of men and to be mothers."[18] For Erik Erikson of Harvard University, woman's mature fulfillment rests on the fact that her somatic design harbors an "inner space" destined to bear the offspring of chosen men, and with it, "a biological, psychological, and ethical commitment to take care of human infancy."[19] We will leave the final word with Joseph Rheingold, a

[16]Both statements are quoted in Stern, "The Womanly Image," p. 88.

[17]Judd Marmor, clinical professor of psychiatry at UCLA, quoted in Stern, "The Womanly Image."

[18]Quoted in Naomi Weisstein, *Kinder, Küche, Kirche as Scientific Law* (Boston: New England Free Press, 1969), p. 1.

[19]Quoted in Weisstein, *Kinder*, p. 1.

psychiatrist at Harvard Medical School: "Woman is nurturance. . . . Anatomy decrees the life of a woman. . . . When women grow up without dread òf their biological function and without subversion by feminist doctrine, and therefore enter upon motherhood with a sense of fulfillment and altruistic sentiment, we shall attain the goal of a good life and a secure world in which to live."[20]

Such conceptions provide new-found rationalizations, then, for sex-role standards and sex-role typing in our society. In our summary we shall rely heavily upon the succinct analysis offered by psychologist Jerome Kagan: these standards dictate to the female that she must feel needed and desired by a man and that her complete fulfillment in life can come only in raising and rearing a family. Dependency, passivity, and conformity is not only permitted, it is encouraged in the girl child. For the male, on the other hand, sex-role standards stress the need to be independent in action, to dominate others, and to be able to control strong emotions, especially fear and helplessness. In America a boy is driven to prove that he is strong and powerful, and secondarily to arouse and gratify a love object. Other primary sex-typed behaviors are aggression—permitted in males, inhibited in females—and intellectual striving—encouraged in males, deprecated in females. A host of minor sex-typed attributes are transmitted in the growing process, and a person's sex-role identity is developed according to how well his biological and psychological characteristics correspond to his or her concept of the ideal male or female. Ambiguity or frailty in this area is recognized as a source of severe stress and anxiety in many.[21]

How are these sex standards learned? Through the family, first of all, and through the education process, the media, the church, and, finally, peer groups. From infancy on, girls and boys receive messages contributing to their typing as either male or female, and usually, from the year two, some awareness of sex identity and sex standards has taken root. It is developed and reinforced at every

[20]Quoted in Weisstein, *Kinder,* p. 1.

[21]Jerome Kagan, "Check One: Male–Female," *Psychology Today*, July 1969, pp. 39–42. See also Jerome Kagan, "Acquisition and Significance of Sex Typing and Sex Role Identity," in M. L. Hoffmann and L. W. Hoffmann, eds., *Review of Child Development Research* (New York: Russell Sage Foundation, 1964), vol. 1.

step of the way from then on—as witness the images of mothers and fathers, boys and girls in the children's literature and textbooks discussed earlier. So subtle and pervasive are our preconceptions of sex attributes that we are most often not aware of how we channel boys and girls into distinct and different directions of development.

An instructive example of just such unconscious channeling is offered by teacher Julie Edwards of Davis, California. Comparing questionnaires submitted to parents of children in a private nursery school, Mrs. Edwards found that parents' approval and disapproval of qualities affecting their children's sociability could be clearly divided along sex lines. Parents of girls stressed their malleability, cooperativeness, and willingness to take direction as their daughters' most valuable characteristics. Disapproval was given to assertiveness and affinity to quarrel. Boys, on the other hand, were praised for being independent, assertive, and inquisitive, and severely put down for being timid and fearful.

The teachers' attitudes were found to correspond very well, indeed. Watching the children play on the outside jungle gym, for instance, teachers would quickly interfere with a little girl having trouble in climbing up to the top: "Take it easy, dear—we'll help you down." But a boy trying the same daring feat would be cheered on: "That's the boy! You can make it if you want to!" Similarly, a girl acting aggressively would be put down for being bossy, while identical behavior in a boy would be dismissed with an easygoing shrug: "That's boys, you know."[22]

These conclusions have been confirmed in other research projects. In one wide-ranging study, *aggression* was found to be the area of behavior in which the greatest sex distinctions were made by parents. Preschool boys were allowed more aggression in their dealings with other children, while girls were rewarded for nonaggressiveness, conformity, and obedience.[23] W. A. Mischel agrees that from early childhood on, dependent behavior is less rewarded for males and physically aggressive behavior less rewarded for females in our culture.[24]

---

[22]Unpublished research, reported at the Conference on Women, University of California at Davis, May 1970.

[23]R. R. Sears, Eleanor Maccoby, and H. Levin, *Patterns of Child Rearing* (Evanston, Ill.: Row, Peterson, 1957), p. 403.

[24]W. A. Mischel, "A Social Learning View of Sex Differences in Behavior," in Eleanor Maccoby, ed., *The Development of Sex Differences* (Stanford, Calif.: Stanford University Press, 1966) p. 75.

Few of us could claim never to have been guilty of such stereotyping in dealing with young boys and girls. Combined with the images projected in their reading material and transmitted through the media, the dictations of sex-role standards are bound to have a powerful impact on the personality development of members of either sex. This goes a long way toward explaining why and how it comes about that girls, for instance, tend to shy away from fields of activities considered adventuresome or intellectually taxing. It also provides clues as to how it comes about that as girls pass puberty, their drive to achieve in fields not recognized as "feminine" goes into drastic decline. Girls are, in fact, superior in academic achievement up to and through high school, and they continue to do comparatively well in college. Yet fewer girl high-achievers than boy high-achievers go on to college and, while there, a very small proportion choose to major in fields like science, mathematics, economics, medicine, and law. Even fewer go on to and complete graduate school. The percentage of advanced degrees earned by women has, in fact, been going down—from 13 percent in 1940 to 11.8 percent in 1963.[25]

Psychologist Matina Horner has shown that, consciously or unconsciously, girls equate intellectual achievement with a loss of femininity and that for girl students the desire to achieve is often contaminated by the *motive to avoid success.*[26] This she defines as "the fear that success in competitive achievement situations will lead to negative consequences, such as unpopularity and loss of femininity."[27] In a fascinating experiment, the standard Thematic Apperception Test, achievement-motivation measures were administered to a sample of boy and girl undergraduates. Over 65 percent of the girls and fewer than 10 percent of the boys showed evidence of the motive to avoid success.

The full extent of sex-typing upon the achievement and career aspirations of women is shown dramatically in a study of college graduates in 1961 conducted by the National Opinion Research Center.[28] The women in the sample showed superior academic

[25]Robert M. Cunningham, Jr., "Some Women Who Made It Offer Insights into Their Problems," *College and University Business,* February 1970, p. 58.
[26]Matina S. Horner, "Women's Will to Fail," *Psychology Today,* November 1969, pp. 36–39, 62.
[27]Horner, p. 38.
[28]James A. Davis and Norman Bradburn, *Great Aspirations: Career Plans of America's June, 1961 College Graduates,* National Opinion Research Center Report No. 82 (September 1961).

performance throughout college, and yet their career aspirations differed markedly from those of the men in the study. Among 33,782 college graduates, 11,000 women expected to pursue careers in elementary and secondary education, but only 285 hoped to enter medicine, law, or engineering.

What must be understood is that the whole socialization process is geared to discourage in girls any involvement and success in "masculine" pursuits, that is, pursuits that require ambition, daring, and inquisitiveness. Not only are such tendencies in girls the occasion for surprise and concern, so that they have to go against the advice and without the approval of most parents, teachers, or peers if they are to persist in their "masculinized" ways, but also there are no female models for them to look to and follow—either in history books or in the educational texts generally. Nor for that matter are there more than a scattering of models in real life— women who have broken out of the imprisoning norms and accepted the challenges of an exciting, though often hostile, male-dominated profession.

There are additional burdens to carry for girls and women chafing under the strains imposed by sex standards. To seek and hold a man and to bear and raise his children is even more than just the ultimate fulfillment for a woman, our sex norms would have her believe. It is also her duty to her fellow humans and to society. To the charge of "penis envy" and "castration complex" that psychology has provided for use against women who choose to challenge male prerogatives, additional accusations of deviancy and destructiveness are leveled at these "masculinized" females from the anchor points of sociology and anthropology. The conventional wisdom of these disciplines would have us believe that the traditional division of roles between the sexes is "natural" and "good" for the society—even, some would add, "inevitable." The implicit assumption underlying functional analysis in social science is that *persistence* in social arrangements is a test of validity, since every institutional phenomenon will be judged on the basis of its contributions to the stability or dynamic equilibrium of a society. Thus the ascription of sex role is considered fundamental to the maintenance and continuance of any society and the particular sex standards and sex typing prevailing over time are therefore *functional,* that is, they contribute to the equilibrium of the society. A sociologist may profess that this is not a value judgment, but the use of such terms as *deviance, marginality,* and *pathology* in the discussion of radical social innovations or of individuals breaking with traditional norms is not without persuasive implications. And naturally, in the context of sex-role development, such labels are applied to women and men who try to transcend the limitations imposed upon them by conventional sex-typing. In the functionalist scheme of analysis, a challenge and attempt at change present a problem and not an opportunity. Adjustment and adaptation to present role structures and insistence on new ones imply a serious degree of pathology in the individual and a potentially destructive case of deviance for the society.

The Heavy Toll of Sexual Conditioning

As a consequence, the girl and boy growing up in America will receive messages throughout their education that reinforce the sex-typing started in infancy. Even in universities, sex standards are not questioned—or were not until very recently. Female students are still primarily oriented toward finding a husband and raising a family—other interests and drives are discouraged and become illegitimate in society's view if and when they threaten to dominate. Society's expectations about the female role dictate to the female student that she be popular, desirable, marriageable, and able and willing to bear children. At the same time, society's dictations of what is desirable in a female preclude the development of independence of mind, intellectual inquisitiveness, assertiveness, and a drive to compete.

Such conditioning, we have to remember, is taking place at a time when egalitarian principles are uniformly recognized in institutions of higher learning and when the whole structure of public education rests on the acceptance of equality of opportunity, without regard to color, race, religion, or sex. The result is confusion, ambivalence, and emotional havoc among girls with talents or intellectual abilities. The result is also a damaged self-image and a decline in self-respect among the vast majority who cannot transcend the narrow stereotypes of behavior proscribed for them. How serious and widespread are these negative feelings among

112   **A New Look at the Silenced Majority**

women is indicated by reports such as a *Fortune* magazine poll showing that more than one-fourth of women wish they had been born in the opposite sex[29] and a study of fourth-graders showing ten times as many girls wishing they could be boys as boys wishing they could be girls.[30] Women inevitably come to internalize the general disesteem in which they are held, as demonstrated by Philip Goldberg in his intriguing study, "Are Women Prejudiced against Other Women?" He found the answer to his question by testing the reaction of women undergraduates to an essay signed alternately by "John McKay" and "Joan McKay." The result, as expected, was that women downgraded the work of professionals of their own sex—not only in traditionally masculine fields, but in traditionally feminine fields as well.[31]

This confirms the fact that women view their differences from men as *deficiencies,* not just as complementary qualities offering equally valuable opportunities. Strikingly, this feeling is also typical among self-conscious minority groups. As Kurt Lewin has shown, group self-hatred is a frequent reaction of a minority-group member to his group affiliation.[32] Personality distortion cannot be escaped, since a person's conception of himself is based on the defining gestures of others. Self-hatred is exhibited by a person's tendency to denigrate other members of the group, or to be scornful of himself. Helen Hacker offers the following insight in her classic study, *Women as a Minority Group:*

> Certainly women have not been immune to the formulations of the female character throughout the ages. From those, to us, deluded creatures who confessed to witchcraft to modern sophisticates who speak disparagingly of the cattiness and disloyalty of women, women reveal the introjection of prevailing attitudes towards them. Like those minority groups whose self-castigation outdoes dominant group derision of them, women frequently exceed men in the violence of their vituperation of their sex.[33]

[29]Quoted in Helen Hacker, "Women as a Minority Group," *Social Forces,* no. 3 (1951):62.
[30]Godwin Wolson, "Psychological Aspects of Sex Roles," in G. B. Watson, ed., *Social Psychology: Issues and Insights* (Philadelphia: Lippincott, 1966), p. 477.
[31]Philip Goldberg, "Are Women Prejudiced against Other Women?" *Trans-Action,* April 1968, pp. 28–31.
[32]Kurt Lewin, "Self-Hatred among Jews," quoted in Hacker, "Women as a Minority Group," p. 61.
[33]Hacker, "Women as a Minority Group."

Even among women professionals, "the pattern of self-hatred and group disparagement is not untypical," as Cynthia Fuchs Epstein points out. Interviews with women lawyers found them frequently saying negative things about other women lawyers, suggesting that they, the others, suffered from personality disturbances, worked to compensate for their failures as mothers and wives, and the like. Nor did the interviewees care to be identified with "women lawyers" as a social category.[34]

Women's low evaluations of their own sex is also indicated by the finding that male babies are preferred over female babies by both parents.[35] Curiously, however, women who are apparently resigned to their traditional feminine roles usually protest their satisfaction with "being women." At the same time, *only 10 percent* of a large sample of housewives surveyed by Gallup would want their daughters to live the same way they have.[36] The remaining 90 percent would want their daughters to get more education and to marry later than they did. Also significant in this context is the disclosure of a 1968 survey that there are nearly 10 million housewives who would like to find some work to supplement their homemaking role.[37] One can only conclude that there is less fulfillment to be found in the traditional feminine assignments than our cultural kingmakers and their loyal female following claim.

Some studies do, in fact, point to a very disturbing gap between reality and the sexist ideology's rosy portrayal of a fully feminine life. Dr. Alan Porter found that wives are sixty times more likely to become depressed than single women. A three-year study of depression among his patients led him to conclude that "married women are prone to the disorder at any time in their lives and relapse is frequent."[38] These findings seem to be confirmed in an authoritative study of employed mothers in America edited by F.

[34]Cynthia Fuchs Epstein, *Woman's Place* (Berkeley: University of California Press, 1970), pp. 26–27.

[35]See, for example, Amitai Etzioni, "Sex Control, Science, and Society," *Science* 161 (1968): 1107–12.

[36]George Gallup and Evan Hill, "The American Woman," *Saturday Evening Post*, December 22, 1962.

[37]Richard J. Schonberger, "Ten Million Housewives Want to Work," *Labor Law Journal* 21, no. 6 (June 1970): 374–79.

[38]A. M. W. Porter, "Depressive Illness in a General Practice: A Demographic Study and a Controlled Trial of Imipramine," *British Medical Journal*, no. 1, (1970): 703–78.

Ivan Nye and Lois W. Hoffmann, which points out that working mothers are less likely than housewives to complain of pains and ailments in different parts of their body and of not feeling healthy enough to carry out things they would like to do. Employed mothers also show more self-acceptance and fewer physical symptoms of distress. They do, however, have doubts about their adequacy as parents.[39] But these, it would seem, result from social pressure rather than from any failure on the part of the working mother. No support was found for the view that working mothers have more difficulty with their children or are more negative in their feelings toward them than stay-at-home mothers.[40]

Another postulate of sexist ideology was disproved by the study "Working Wives and Family Happiness" by sociologists Susan Orden and Norman Bradburn. In sexist folklore, it is the wife and mother who *wants* to work who is to be deplored. Her desire is suspect and indicative of a less-than-perfect adjustment to the proper nurturant role. For her to work because of economic need is, however, OK. Yet the two sociologists found that families of women who work because they *want* to are distinctly better off emotionally than families of women who work because they *have* to.[41]

But so powerful is the ideology of sexism, so ubiquitous and clamorous its doctrine, that despite all evidence to the contrary women themselves have been emotionally entrapped in it. No greater tribute could be made to its persuasiveness than the continued insistence on the part of many women that all they want in life is wifely happiness and maternal fulfillment. The contrast in horizons and ambitions between women and men is here immediate and striking. What would we think, after all, of a man who professed such limited goals? For men it is human fulfillment that is to be sought—not just satisfaction in marriage and fatherhood. But, then, men are *persons*, individuals with needs and interests and drives that transcend their sex role. Women, it would seem, do not

[39]Ivan F. Nye and Lois W. Hoffman, eds., *The Employed Mother in America* (Chicago: Rand McNally, 1963), p. 344.

[40]Nye and Hoffman, p. 330.

[41]Quoted in Elizabeth Janeway, "Happiness and the Right to Choose," *Atlantic Monthly*, March 1970, pp. 118–23.

quite make it into that exalted category—or so sexist ideology would have it.

Penis Envy and Other Hazy Theories

Our assertion that this body of beliefs, well integrated and designed to guide social activity, is a full-fledged ideology requires for its validity that we show it to rest on assumptions that are not reliably tested, but to some degree are accepted on faith. Well, then, what is known about the assumptions concerning woman's nature and her destiny in human society? Can they be said to be confirmed through the application of scientific method? Is there sufficient empirical data to support the far-reaching conclusions drawn by many psychologists, sociologists, and anthropologists?

We can start (as, in a sense, did the rest of these analysts) with Freud. The image of woman projected by the older Freudian school of psychoanalysis is that of a passive, masochistic, and narcissistic being. Freud's theory of woman's psychology was based on his observation of a universal feminine tendency, which he traced to early childhood experiences. This is "penis envy," which—according to Freud—inevitably takes possession of unsuspecting little girls as soon as they observe "the penis of a brother and playmate, strikingly visible and of large proportions." Naturally, to Freud, they "at once recognize it as the superior counterpart of their own small and inconspicuous organ,"[42] and from this moment on a feeling of impotence will never leave the girl until her quest for the missing penis is sublimated in maternity. This presents fulfillment, then, "especially so if the baby is a little boy who brings the longed-for penis with him."[43]

The double blow dealt to woman here is quite a stunner, indeed. With such a handicap, it stands to reason that there is little use for her to aspire to equality with man. Every instance of dissatisfaction and rebellion can be put down to envy, to the desire to "castrate" a man. And then, as sublime maternity (a feat to be accomplished

[42]Sigmund Freud, "Some Psychological Consequences of the Anatomical Distinctions between the Sexes," *Collected Papers* (New York: Basic Books, 159), 5:190.

[43]Sigmund Freud, *Three Contributions to the Theory of Sex* (New York: Dutton, 1962), p. 127.

only with the cooperation of a man, mind) promises to relieve her of anxiety and frustration, it turns out that the product has to be male for ultimate fulfillment to be achieved!

Note, then, the "evidence" presented by Freud for confirmation of this most ambitious theory: He *observed*—and he *speculated*. There is, needless to say, no way to empirically test whether the phenomenon called "penis envy" has the universality and far-reaching implications claimed by Freud or, indeed, if it even exists. Girls lack the equipment in question, it is true, but then boys do not share in the complementary equipment of girls, either, and no theory has been put forth concerning an all-important "vagina envy" among the male sex. Indeed, to grown women the thought is rather ludicrous that a physiognomic part so vulnerable to damage, so unresponsive to command, and so awkwardly placed in terms of potential hurt and embarrassment should be something to want to have placed on one's own body.

The lack of such desire is indeed verified by the clinical experiences of psychiatrists like Clara Thompson[44] and Joseph B. Furst.[45] As Dr. Furst points out, the Freudian explanation is no explanation at all. It is merely a huge argument in a circle, equivalent to saying that women have problems because they are not men.

It is the social context, we now know, that shapes and determines personality development. What a person does and who he believes himself to be will, as Naomi Weisstein points out, in general be "a function of what people around him expect him to be and what the overall situation in which he is acting implies he is."[46] Thus when women are found to be passive and narcissistic, such qualities should not be attributed, in the first place, to anything but the particular social conditioning women have been subject to and the social environment in which they continue to live. For these characteristics to be proved "basic" and inherent, we need more than mere theorizing about instinctual drives and bland assertions that biology is destiny. We need, for instance, documentation that these are the predominant characteristics of women in all known human societies over time and/or that women who do not possess them are

---

[44]Clara Thompson, "Penis Envy," *Psychology* 6, no. 2 (May 1943).

[45]Joseph B. Furst, *The Neurotic and His Inner and Outer World* (New York: Citadel Press, 1954), p. 81.

[46]Weisstein, *Kinder*, p. 3.

not in possession of female physical characteristics and capabilities.

But such documentation has never been presented. On the contrary, what we have learned is that there are marked differences among cultures in the specific personality characteristics ascribed to women and men, as there are in the degree of differentiation between the two sex roles. In her now classic study, *Sex and Temperament in Three Primitive Societies,* Margaret Mead effectively demonstrated that in one society, the Mundugumor, both men and women tend to be ruthless, aggressive, severe, and unresponsive; in another, the Arapesh, both men and women had characteristics assumed in the West to be feminine—both sexes were unaggressive, cooperative, and responsive to the needs of others; and in the third society, the Tchambuli, the personality characteristics are the reverse of what we consider "natural"—women are dominant, impersonal, and managing and men are emotionally dependent and less responsible.[47] Historians as well as anthropologists have come up with evidence of matriarchal societies in the past, with indications that women exhibited anything but passive tendencies in their social relationships. Some sociologists, as well, have blasted the notion that there is a single set of characteristics defining women. In many places, it is pointed out, it is men who are thought to be emotional, sensitive, and intuitive, whereas women are thought to be cool and calculating. Modern Iran is a prominent example.[48] Scholars like Karen Horney, Erich Fromm, and Viola Klein have criticized the image of woman created by Freud and his followers. Says Viola Klein in *The Feminine Character:* "The realization that in different societies women fulfill different social functions, and accordingly display different attitudes and mental characteristics, has shattered the idea of the all-powerful influence of anatomy and biological traits on character traits."[49]

An example, now amusing, of the shallowness and fault in Freudian theorizing is the widely accepted notion, prominent in Freudian thought, that women have less sexual drive than men. Both this misconception and another Freudian maxim, that the

[47]Margaret Mead, *Sex and Temperament in Three Primitive Societies* (New York: Morrow, 1935).

[48]Bernice C. Sachs, "Woman's Destiny: Choice or Chance," *Journal of the American Medical Women's Association* 20, no. 8 (August 1965): 733–38.

[49]Quoted in Sachs, p. 733.

vagina orgasm is the only mature orgasm, have been exposed as bunk by the painstaking research in recent scholarship, in particular by Masters and Johnson in their massive study *Human Sexual Response*.[50] Women are, if anything, sexually superior to men in that they are capable of enjoying an infinite number of orgasms and are not dependent on the response of any one organ to enter into intercourse. Also, contrary to the idea that equality between the sexes would feminize men and masculinize women, thereby threatening satisfying sexual relationships, psychologist Abraham Maslow found after several studies that the more "dominant" the woman, the greater her enjoyment of sexuality, the greater her ability to give herself freely in love.[51] Alice S. Rossi summarizes his findings thus: "Women with dominance feelings were free to be completely themselves, and this was crucial for their full expression in sex. They were not feminine in the traditional sense, but enjoyed sexual fulfillment to a much greater degree than the conventionally feminine women he studied."[52] This fact is corroborated by Masters and Johnson. Yet to Freudians like Dr. Marie Robinson, famed for her *Power of Sexual Surrender*, the driving, competitive woman who is successful in the business world is "masculinized," and therefore *frigid.*[53] As to the immaturity of clitoral orgasm, considered by Freud a sign of abortive emotional development in a woman, evidence is now in from many sources that there is but one kind of orgasm, the clitoral. The Freudian distinction is false to begin with.[54]

Need we explore further this maze of hazy theories and unfounded assumptions to show that beliefs about woman's nature and destiny are founded more on faith than on scientific evidence? More rigorous dissections of this web of myths have recently been offered by Naomi Weisstein, Anne Koedt, and Kate Millett.[55]

[50]W. H. Masters and Virginia Johnson, *Human Sexual Response* (Boston: Little, Brown, 1966).

[51]A. H. Maslow, "Dominance, Personality, and Social Behavior in Women," *Journal of Social Psychology*, no. 10 (1939): 3–39.

[52]Alice S. Rossi, "Inequality between the Sexes," in R. J. Lifton, ed., *The Woman in America* (Boston: Houghton Mifflin, 1964), p. 139.

[53]Quoted in Stern, "The Womanly Image," p. 177.

[54]See, for example, Masters and Johnson, *Human Sexual Response*, and Anne Koedt, *The Myth of the Vaginal Orgasm* (Boston: New England Free Press, 1969).

[55]See Weisstein, *Kinder;* Koedt, *The Myth of the Vaginal Orgasm;* and Kate Millett, *Sexual Politics* (New York: Doubleday, 1970), pp. 157–235.

Thus, in the conclusion of psychologist Naomi Weisstein: "Psychology has nothing to say about what women are really like, what they need and what they want, essentially, because psychology does not know."[56] Jo Ann Gardner, president of the Association for Women Psychologists, essentially concurs: psychotherapists have reinforced the standard sexual stereotypes of the society. They are therefore useless, or worse than useless, to women with emotional problems or neurotic disturbances. Their concept of a mentally healthy female is that of someone "passive, emotional, dependent, less competitive, nonobjective, submissive, and more easily influenced—like the Negro stereotype. . . . With the help of Freudian concepts, the therapists are doing to women just what they are doing to blacks."[57]

The real and obvious differences between men and women—in physical size, in muscular strength, and in physiognomy in general—would appear to be of less and less consequence in terms of abilities and achievement as technology and civilization continue to advance. There are relatively few jobs left that require physical strength and there are likely to be even fewer as years go by. And whereas childbearing will remain an exclusive function of women and childrearing may continue as a predominantly feminine vocation, these tasks no longer consume more than a relatively small portion of a woman's life. The evidence of testing now points to woman's intelligence and talents being no less than those of man's—the psychological differences observed are to a very great extent acquired rather than innate. We do not, in the end, know what femininity is, or indeed if there really exists such a cluster of traits and trends that are not mainly derivatives of cultural forms.

Like all ideologies, the sexist ideology supports a structure that leans more heavily on some groups than on others. It is, however, too simple to conclude that women are the sole victims and to stop short of further exploration into the costs of sexism. A system as elaborate as this one and requiring for its support such ambitious rationalizations is likely to damage more than the lives within its "under class."

We shall proceed to explore just what and who else are suffering.

[56]Weisstein, *Kinder*, p. 3.
[57]Jo Ann E. Gardner and Charles W. Thomas (with George Harris), "Different Strokes for Different Folks," *Psychology Today*, May 1970, p. 53.

seven

Democracy
and Other Victims

Social structure, socialization process, and ideology all interact to create a system in which women are deprived of their full humanity and shortchanged of their just share of social and economic benefits. This system, like all others, is ruled through politics; that is, it requires for its sustenance and perpetuation a political structure through which demands can be processed and from which commands can come forth and be implemented. The peculiarity in the situation of women in America is, as suggested earlier, that although they constitute a potential voting majority of this democracy, they have only lately come around to *using politics* to change the institutional forms of sexism and thereby improve their own life chances. By raising demands and by organizing to apply pressure on the political system, women have an excellent chance to change and end most forms of discrimination and oppression applying to them. In doing that they would, we will suggest, also change the very quality of American life and significantly upgrade the tone and character of our political dialogue. They might indeed make democracy a social and not just a political reality in America.

We should, by now, have a fair insight into the reasons for women's lack of efficacy in the political arena. The belief in women's innate inferiority and unsuitability for certain types of activities is the greatest obstacle facing those who would organize women. Male chauvinsim may still create the greatest barriers, but women's acceptance of the rightness of their own inferior status makes them easy to control. As we have seen, "the entire society is geared to socialize women to believe in and adopt as immutable necessity their traditional and inferior role."[1] The values and postulates of sexist ideology appear to be quite effectively internalized in most women.

The question that must be raised at this point is this: *What does it do to a democracy*[2] to have half of its citizenry accept self-definitions that are bound to make their exercise of political rights and duties more difficult? Dependency, passivity, and conformity are all strongly endorsed and effectively cultivated feminine traits. How do they conform to the requirements of democratic citizenship? Is it possible that our stereotype of femininity and our ideal of womanhood come to constitute serious interference with a woman's positive orientation to and involvement with politics? Beyond that, what likely loss is endured by this nation as a consequence of the differential input into the system by half of its citizenry?

First, let us briefly examine what classical democratic theorists have had to say about the personal qualities called for in members of a democratic society. Although their conceptions of democracy do not always agree, they all join in the emphasis on popular participation in governing, either through elaborate systems of representation, as favored by James Madison, or by a direct and extensive involvement of all citizens, as suggested by Thomas Jefferson. The ideal is well stated by John Dewey: "The keynote of democracy as a way of life may be expressed as the necessity for the participation of every human being in the formation of values that regulate the living of men together."[3] Not only is the involvement of citizens in political affairs necessary to ensure fair and acceptable policy outcomes, it is also desired for what it can contribute to individual self-development. Political activity, to these theorists, offers un-

[1]Marlene Dixon, *Why Women's Liberation?* (San Francisco: Bay Area Radical Education Project, 1969), p. 4.

[2]We shall come to grips with the problem of defining *democracy* later in this chapter. Meanwhile, we shall simply rely on the ideal conception of democracy as a system where individuals participate in the decisions that affect their lives.

[3]John Dewey, "Democracy and Educational Administration," *School and Society*, April 3, 1937; quoted in Thomas R. Dye and L. Harmon Zeigler, *The Irony of Democracy* (Belmont, Calif.: Wadsworth, 1970), p. 6.

rivaled opportunities for citizens to gain in knowledge and understanding and to acquire a sense of social responsibility. According to John Stuart Mill, the first question to ask concerning a particular form of government is: "What sort of human beings can be formed under such a regime? What development can either their thinking or active faculties attain under it?"[4]

Awareness, responsibility, and self-reliance are all considered essential qualities for the proper functioning of democracy and, at the same time, qualities desirable enough in themselves to choose the governmental form that would best foster them. The worth and dignity and creative capacity of each individual is assumed; it is this that makes possible a government of broad participation and maximum self-direction. The aim of government, on the other hand, is precisely the production of citizens responsible enough and capable enough to play this role. Neither Mill nor Jefferson believed that equality of talents and skills could ever come about, but they, like other democratic theorists, affirmed the moral worth of each individual and both the justice and necessity of everyone having a right to take part in the conflict over allocation of values in a society. Only broad participation could ensure that persons qualified for leadership would be found and selected and only active involvement in politics by all citizens would prevent undue power—the power that corrupts—from coming into the hands of a few. For Madison, it was not just the tyranny of minorities, but also that of a majority that posed a danger to human development. But for him, too, the fostering of rationality, responsibility, and awareness in citizens was desirable, even if not always possible.

The contrast between these highly praised attributes and the characteristics of the conventionally "feminine" woman is as striking as it is immediately apparent. Sweetness, passivity, and helplessness may be appealing qualities in a variety of situations, but the political is *not* one of them. A woman whose self-concept is entirely what sexist ideology would have it be is not likely to make independent judgments, to voice her opinions, or to take on political responsibilities. Given the fact that intellectual inquisitiveness is also ruled out as an attribute of femininity, she is likely to feel discouraged from acquiring special knowledge of and consciousness about

[4]John Stuart Mill, *Representative Government*, quoted in Dye and Zeigler, p. 7.

political issues. For her, a sophisticated and consistent use of ideological concepts is apt to conflict with what she has been taught are attractive personality features in a woman. A principled vote, that is, a vote cast on the basis of political ideology, will consequently not be her contribution to the democratic process.

To run for office—to compete against a man in an arena that has for so long been a male preserve—must appear like a total improbability and an outrageous idea to the "feminine" woman. If she still has a husband and children, this in itself is sufficient reason for her to abhor any role but her presently "proper" ones. Even without them, her acceptance of what sexist ideology offers as the image of ideal womanhood will very effectively prevent her from taking on this particular responsibility of democratic citizens—to seek, fight for, and accept the role of leader where occasions call for it. Nor is she likely to be an "opinion leader" in her own peer group; both her own self-concept and the reluctance of others to accept political expertise in a woman get in the way of her exercising political influence in this manner.

It is not too much to say, then, that to the extent it has taken hold, the effect of sexist ideology has been to disarm the American woman politically and also to deprive American democracy of the potentially informed and intelligent contributions of more than half of its citizenry. From the point of view of classic democratic theory, this is clearly disastrous. The model of citizen participation and responsibility posed here cannot be approximated as long as current sex standards and sex typing present serious obstacles to women's entrance into the political arena.

Let us, then, examine the findings of voting experts and opinion researchers to ascertain whether our presumptions concerning the effect of sexist ideology can be affirmed. For the moment we shall leave aside the question, raised by the pluralist school in American political science, of whether the demands imposed by classic theorists on the citizens of a democracy are realistic and at all feasible. We need to know, first, whether there are discernible and significant differences in the way men and women in our society perceive politics and their own role within it. We need to know also how these perceptions influence the choices made by women at the polls and what difference, if any, this makes in likely policy outcomes over time.

The Female Citizen

In 1937 an authority on political behavior concluded that "at every social level women vote less than men."[5] The difference in election turnout between the sexes has grown less significant as the years have passed, until in the national election of 1972 it was not more than 6 percent. In 1948 and 1954, however, there were still 10 percent more men than women exercising the right of franchise.[6] As stated earlier, the gap is by no means large enough to explain the near-absence of women in elective offices on all levels of government, but it does suggest a lesser political involvement on the part of women generally. Apparently there is at least one group of women who experience a lesser social pressure to vote than men do. Interestingly enough, although women score just as high in approval of the system and attachment to the nation, their sense of *citizen duty* is at the same time somewhat lower than that of men. This leads Robert Lane, for one, to speculate that, for a good portion of the female nonvoters, it is the conventional views of the proper female role that interfere with use of the franchise.[7] Such an impression is confirmed by the finding that we get the sharpest differentiation in voting turnout between men and women in the geographical areas and on the socioeconomic levels where sex-typing is the most rigid.

In the South, in rural areas, and among people with only grade-school education, women make use of the ballot significantly less than they do in other localities and situations.[8] Lane quotes some of these nonvoters: "Voting is for men." "I think men should do the voting and women stay home and take care of their work." "A woman's place is in the home. Leave politics to the men."[9]

Although this particular cluster of phenomena—greater ratios of nonvoting among the least educated and poorest women in the population—may have a very serious effect on policy outcomes, the

---

[5] Herbert Tingsten, *Political Behavior Studies in Election Statistics* (London: P. S. King, 1937), p. 29.

[6] Robert E. Lane, *Political Life* (Glencoe, Ill.: Free Press, 1959), p. 210.

[7] Lane, pp. 210–12.

[8] Angus Campbell, Philip E. Converse, Warren E. Miller, and Donald E. Stokes, *The American Voter* (Ann Arbor, Mich.: Survey Research Center, University of Michigan, 1960), pp. 486–92.

[9] Lane, *Political Life,* p. 211.

distinction between male and female political orientations can be more clearly shown by testing the sets of expectations developed by each sex toward the political system and their own role within it. This is where differences derived from sex-typing are most likely to show up and where the deviance from the classic democratic models could be most serious. Effective political activity in a democracy requires both knowledge of issues, candidates, and processes and a certain competence in presenting one's views to political figures. A person's self-concept will have a great deal to do with his or her inclination and ability to acquire these necessary skills. We would expect women to generally rate lower than men in this area, given our cultural preference for nonintellectuality and passive compliance in females. Issue-oriented, politically sophisticated, and assertive citizens may be just what we need in this democracy—but as sexist ideology would prescribe, they had better not be women.

And so it is, as we examine the studies now available on this very important problem. Sex-typing and sex standards appear to affect political orientations from grade school on. The self-concepts of boys are clearly more appropriate for issue orientation and active political involvement. Both girls and boys, for instance, list their father more often than their mother as the source of political information and advice.[10] And girls—it is generally accepted—learn their sex role by imitating their mothers. In voting literature, there are also recurrent reports of male political dominance in the family.[11] As could be expected, therefore, boys are both more interested in political stories and figures and better informed about them than are girls. The child's awareness of male political specialization is surely an important factor here—the nearly total absense of women models in history and government textbooks and in contemporary political life must be assumed to reinforce the girl's impression that "politics is not for women."

Among adults, the sharpest and most consistent differences between the sexes turn up in regard to the sense of political efficacy. Men are more likely to feel that they can cope with the complexities of politics and to believe that their participation carries some weight in the political process. The conclusion is clear, then, that

[10]Fred E. Greenstein, "Sex-related Political Differences in Childhood," *Journal of Politics*, May 1961, pp. 353–72.
[11]Greenstein, p. 364.

although "moralistic values about citizen participation in democratic government have been bred in women as in men, what has been less adequately transmitted to the woman is a sense of some personal competence vis-à-vis the political world."[12]

Such a feeling of competence is, as noted earlier, an important prerequisite for effective political involvement in a democracy. But the greatest damage to democratic politics may yet come from the pervasive influence of sex-role definitions on the level of political sophistication among women. The ability to conceptualize, identify, and distinguish ideological abstractions, or at the very least group interests, is a necessary quality for democratic citizenship, according to our classic democratic theorists. Here again women were found to score significantly lower than men and, again, the differences were larger the less the amount of formal education.[13] Women whose education has been on the grade-school level, where sex-typing is the most rigid, turn out to have the most impoverished level of concept formation.

These early findings are at least partially confirmed in a number of attitude surveys to date. Women respondents frequently fall into the "no response" or "no opinion" categories at a higher rate than men.

Women are also handicapped in regard to candidate recognition. The Harris Poll of July 1970 found 62 percent of men but only 53 percent of women able to identify the senators of their state. The difference was even larger as respondents were asked to identify the parties of their representatives in the Senate; here only 47 percent of women were able to give the correct answer as against 60 percent of the men.[14]

It must be added that women constitute by far the largest group within the "ticket splitters"—a growing and increasingly important phenomenon in our electoral process. To students of political behavior, this does not reflect well on the political perceptions of the female half of the nation. The great majority of these "fickle" voters—those who remain uncommitted to a party and who tend to

---

[12]Campbell, et al., *The American Voter*, p. 491. This conclusion is confirmed in a recent study by Maureen Fiedler, "The Participation of Women in American Politics," presented at the American Political Science Associations Conference in San Francisco, September 1975.

[13]Campbell et al., *The American Voter*, p. 492.

[14]Louis Harris Poll, July 1970.

switch their votes from election to election or within one election, pick candidates "for the office" and not from the party—are quite simply political outsiders. They are the people, by and large, who neither care much nor know much about politics.[15] According to a national sampling in 1967 by Market Opinion Research, 57.2 percent of the ticket splitters were female, 42.8 percent male.

Two important consequences may flow from this constellation of attitudes. The lesser involvement of women and their lesser sense of efficacy and political sophistication will contribute to the decline in issue orientation and partisanship among candidates in office. Our political dialogue in general will suffer. Also, the stronger emphasis on moral issues among the typically "feminine" women, consonant with their nurturant roles, may lead to an excessive focus on the superficial and less relevant aspects of politics. In the opinion of some scholars, it is likely to breed somewhat greater intolerance and fear of conflict.[16]

To the extent, then, that American women are politically disarmed by sex-role stereotyping and conditioning, the model of citizen participation, awareness, and responsibility posed in classic democratic theory cannot be approximated. Habitual compliance, passivity, and dependence are the very qualities we do not want in our citizens. If these attributes are combined with ignorance of issues and of democratic procedural values, it can make for quite a combustible mixture in a crisis situation, as scholars have shown us. In the end, the "feminine" citizen—the woman whose attitudes and orientation to politics is totally what the female role model would have it be—may be a threat and not an asset to democracy.

The Governing Elites

But then, women are not alone in being unable to measure up to the ideal of democratic citizenship posed by some of our forefathers. As voting analysis and opinion research have made abundantly clear, the American voter in general, male or female, falls far short of these standards. Issue consciousness is limited to a small group of the population; there is widespread political apathy

---

[15]J. D. Barber, *Citizen Politics* (Chicago: Markham, 1969).
[16]See Lane, *Political Life,* and Samuel Stouffer, *Communism, Conformity, and Civil Liberties* (New York: Doubleday, 1955).

among many sectors of the public; and there is startling little understanding of democratic values and procedures.[17] Yet to pluralist
theorists of democracy[18] this poses no great problem, for the system is saved by political elites who share a consensus on fundamental democratic values and who constitute the politically active and
influential segment of the society. In *their* hands, democracy is safe.
The competition between these elites ensures the citizens' right of
participation; elite behavior can be influenced by making choices
between competing elites in elections. Democratic values are affirmed also by the fact that these elites are not closed and that new
groups can gain access to elite positions. Pluralists are sometimes
accused of slighting the problem of political apathy and alienation
and, equally, of denigrating the role of social movements and political radicals.[19] In context of their explanatory scheme, it is a high
degree of involvement and not apathy on the part of citizens that
poses a problem. Given the lack of political sophistication and appreciation of democratic values among Americans today, it is better
that they stay quiescent and leave political involvement and governing to the elites.

To pluralists, consequently, the key problem in politics becomes
that of *who governs?* Such is, indeed, the title of the most influential
book coming out of this school.[20] The viability of pluralist democracy depends to a great extent on whether individuals fit to govern
will be found in any situation. The successful politician, adept at
negotiation and bargaining, can find formulas for compromise that
will keep controversies from becoming too hot and conflict too
divisive. This is crucial for the maintenance of stability and the
preservation of democratic freedoms. But the individuals qualified
to take on such delicate and difficult tasks are few and far between:

[17]See, for example, Campbell et al., *The American Voter;* and Stouffer, *Communism,
Conformity, and Civil Liberties.* See also Herbert McClosky, "Consensus and Ideology
in American Politics," *American Political Science Review* 58, no. 2 (1964):361–82; and
Lane, *Political Life.*

[18]Foremost among these are Robert A. Dahl, Nelson Polsby, Charles Lindblom,
and Aaron Wildavsky.

[19]See, for example, Lane Davis, "The Cost of Realism: Contemporary Restate-
ments of Democracy," *Western Political Quarterly* 17 (1964); 37–46; Peter Bachrach
and Morton S. Baratz, "The Two Faces of Power," *American Political Science Review*
56 (1962): 947–52; and Jack L. Walker, "A Critique of the Elitist Theory of Democracy," *American Political Science Review* 60, no. 2 (1966): 285–96.

[20]Robert Dahl, *Who Governs?* (New Haven: Yale University Press, 1961).

one common estimate is that they amount to no more than about 2 percent of the population. And this tiny minority, on whom rests the responsibility of governing, must be constantly replenished.

Thus it would seem that the incapacities our sexist ideology aims to induce in half of our citizenry is a matter of grave concern for pluralist theories as well as for those of the classic democratic schools. We are being deprived, quite simply, of the potential political talents and skills to be found among these 53.7 percent of eligible voters. As long as sex standards and sex-typing continue in their present forms, there is but little chance that women naturally endowed with the qualities needed for governing will be added to the pool of new recruits. This can only be viewed as a great loss, given the small dimensions and central importance of the latter. For pluralists and for classic democratic theorists alike, sexist ideology presents a formidable obstacle to the creation and/or maintenance of a viable democracy.

The "John Wayne Syndrome": In and out of Politics

The common ideal of manhood in America may also constitute a problem—at times a formidable one—to the pursuit of rational, cautious, and humane policies in this republic. Maleness, as defined by our sex standards, requires strength, daring, independence, and a certain brusqueness in tone and manner. This standard carries with it a tolerance even admiration for physically aggressive behavior. Boys are usually encouraged to fight back—no matter what the odds; to accept defeat or to recognize one's weakness in a battle becomes very difficult for a young male socialized in our culture. Retreat in particular carries with it a social stigma that is painful to bear for the individual involved. The result appears to be that a good many American men suffer from what has been called the "John Wayne syndrome"—the belief that a punch in the nose will set everything right! Although women, with their greater compliance with authority and attachment to the system and governmental figures, may be more prone to accept the conspiracy theories so frequently offered to explain away the problems of the nation, men, on the other hand, are likely to insist on pursuing policies shown to be unfruitful and even detrimental, on the basis of their fear of appearing weak or their distaste for retreating from a fight. Some rather astounding statements from contemporary leaders come to mind: President Lyndon B. Johnson, reacting to the Dominican Republic revolt of 1965, refused to "sit in his rocking chair" and allow Communists to take over another country in Latin America—and so the Marines were sent in. President Nixon, in 1969, reacting to demands for a pullout of American troops in Vietnam, refused to be the first American president in history to accept defeat in a war and so the troops had to fight on for three more years, though the end was obvious as it was bitter. There was also our brave Senator Barry Goldwater who wanted the president, when negotiating with the Soviets, to speak "with the nukes rattling in his pockets." Not to mention the late Congressman Mendell Rivers, who professed no fear of world nuclear disaster as long as the new Adam and Eve be American! And the greatest diplomat in recent U.S. history Secretary of State Henry Kissinger has confessed that his favorite image of himself is that of a lone cowboy riding into a hostile town.

What is peculiar and disturbing about such assertions is what they reveal about the motives guiding some of our leaders. Policies appear to be pursued not just for "reasons of state," but for reasons of *pride*—a pride that can only come from an acceptance of the ideals of manhood imposed upon us by sexist ideology. It is striking that as late as fall 1970—with our Vietnam policy so obviously defunct—all of 45 percent of American men opposed the proposal to bring our troops home by the end of 1971. That policy was then favored by 54 percent of the women. By 1972 the sex gap on this issue had widened: 70 percent of the women versus 54 percent of the men would withdraw all troops from Vietnam by the end of that year.[21] In regard to the "bombing for peace"(!) issue, it is also notable that 52 percent of the men polled favored the resumption of bombing North Vietnam in the fall of 1972, with only 30 percent of women approving.

Similar differences between the sexes show up in regard to the issues of granting amnesty to draft evaders and tougher penalties for lawbreakers, the death penalty in particular. Far more women than men reveal that they feel threatened by crime. In March 1972, the Gallup Poll found 58 percent of women versus 20 percent of

[21]Gallup Polls, September 1970, August 1972, and September 1972. All reported in the *San Francisco Chronicle*.

men saying they would be afraid to walk at night in an area "around here"; 41 percent of women versus 29 percent of men also agreed that that there was *more* crime in their areas than there had been in the previous year. In spite of these perceptions, only 55 percent of the women versus 73 percent of the men found the courts "not harsh enough" in dealing with criminals. And in regard to the question of the death penalty that same month, only 45 percent of women versus 55 percent of men declared themselves in favor of it.[22]

The lesser inclination to "toughness" and desire for retribution on the part of women is shown quite clearly in a poll on the death penalty conducted by the Louis Harris organization in June 1973. The question posed was: "Suppose it could be proved to your satisfaction that the death penalty was not more effective than prison sentences in keeping other people from committing crimes such as murder, would you be in favor of the death penalty or would you oppose it?" It turned out that 40 percent of men versus 31 percent of women still wanted the death penalty—after the only rational argument for its maintenance had been eliminated.[23]

These findings confirm that not only women, but men as well are subject to sex-role dictates in their political behavior. Results in the latter poll, in particular, can only be interpreted in light of the compulsion toward toughness and fear of "softness" inherent in the masculine sex role in our society. A study of the *"male role"* in politics may be long overdue!

The point to be emphasized here is that the personality characteristics associated with proper femininity and manliness are arbitrarily assigned to each sex without regard to the very complex and wide-ranging differences inherent in the members of both. There are men who find it very difficult to be strong, independent, and aggressive, just as there are women who develop such attributes with comparative ease. But for either, the deviation from sex norms causes anxiety and severe emotional stress. One consequence of doubts or recognition of failure in the ability to live up to the approved sex standards of society is overcompensation in some area of behavior clearly associated in one's mind with what is typical of one's own sex. For men, this is more often than not aggressive-

[22]Gallup Poll, March 1972.
[23]Louis Harris Poll, June 1973.

ness. The "he-man" image—in mass media as well as literature—is that of the silent, strong men who can deal with recalcitrants and settle most problems through the application of physical force. The attitudes of men insecure in their feelings of "masculinity" are bound to be influenced by this incessant and excessive emphasis on aggressiveness in the male culture heroes. This may, indeed, go a long way toward explaining the prevalence of violence in American society—and the fact that by far most criminally violent behavior here is committed by men.

For women, compensation is likely to come in widely different aspects of behavior. Given the favored image of femininity flashed on screens and brandished in ads, where the female—whether as glamour girl or homemaker—orients her activities and her whole life around the man, a woman finding herself lacking in the supposed feminine attributes may make up for it by insisting, against all evidence, that she is only interested in loving and serving a man. Thus some women prominent in fields requiring just the assertiveness, ambition, and toughness that supposedly makes them inaccessible to females will declare that they are *really* just interested in making their men happy. Or women obviously dominant in a marriage or an erotic relationship will try to save their "femininity" by insisting that their only place is in the home. Again, we are reminded of some surprising statements by women who have attained fame and wealth at their own behest. Television personality Arlene Francis, for one, continuously fighting for a place in a field beset with difficulties and obstacles to women, still persisted for years in declaring that women were happiest and most fulfilled as housewives. Veteran actresses, like Rosalind Russell, in a profession that takes not just talent but usually both the keenest ambition and the rawest of guts, were often heard declaring that they would gladly give it all up for the man of their choice anytime he asks for that. How lucky, then, that he doesn't—or that other reasons can be found for the divorces so common in the profession. Jacqueline Bisset, of recent movie fame, emphatically stated that what she really liked to do was cook and clean for her man. With an income of $100,000 or more yearly, her compelling need to do that can well be imagined. Shirley Temple Black, United States representative to the United Nations in 1970 and for years active on her own in hard and bitterly fought political campaigns, declared while on a speaking tour in the fall of 1970 that she was not interested in "women's liberation"; she preferred the "protective arms of her husband" around her. Absenting herself from those as often as she does, she must be sorely bereaved indeed.

This is *not* just amusing. The psychological costs imposed by sexist ideology are difficult to bear for both men and women. The more rigid the sex-typing and the more artificial the standards, the more the members of both sexes have to struggle with insecurities and guilt induced by traits and talents not compatible with what is expected of them. And the more stifled their potential and thwarted their development, the more frustrations and hidden resentments will come into play. The consequences—for individual as well as family happiness—can be devastating. For society, just as for democratic politics, the effect is clearly negative. A variety of social disturbances—neuroticism among housewives, criminal aggressiveness among males, rampant homosexuality, political apathy and rigidity in some sectors of the public—all can be traced to or are most likely associated with the impositions of sexist ideology. The nation loses a great deal, moreover, in the underutilization of its women in the political sector. And it loses most painfully in the poverty affecting self-supporting mothers and their children because of the gross inequities in pay and opportunities for women on the job market.

Special attention should be paid to the psychological burdens borne by men in a sexist society. As Dr. Joseph B. Furst points out, their greater freedom and opportunity are not unmixed blessings.[24] What it means in practice is that too much responsibility and too heavy burdens may be laid upon the man or assumed by him as a matter of course. The prescribed relationship between husband and wife calls for him to carry the entire financial burden of supporting a family. This often means that he cannot make himself break out of an occupation that he hates. If his wife has to work despite all of his efforts, he is likely to feel it as a terrible humiliation. A persistent anxiety will be present for the man with no guaranteed job security and a pervasive frustration for the many who continue at the treadmill while chafing at the bonds. A

[24] Joseph B. Furst, *The Neurotic and His Inner and Outer Worlds* (New York: Citadel Press, 1954), p. 87.

relaxation in sex standards, on the other hand, might permit men to encourage their wives to go to work when financial or personal needs call for it.

It is rather too much to bear for one individual to have to be ever supportive, resourceful, strong, and brave without showing signs of very human frailties and fears. The effect is often hostility to women and a rigidity of attitude and manners in erotic situations that gets in the way of love relationships. Sensitivity, tenderness, a willingness to fully share are *not* qualities often noted in the American man. Yet these are the qualities women seem to want, if we are to trust reports published by themselves and their analysts. Companionship and affection are more important than ever to marital happiness. But the man induced to accept "the cowboy syndrome" will be unable to fulfill the expectations of his wife.

What we are referring to here is the dominance of the "strong and silent" male model in our folk culture. As sociologist Charles W. Peck comments, John Wayne can't express his feelings toward women.[25] And James Bond doesn't have any. These are the two figures that have come to represent the male sex role in America. The consequences, Dr. Peck points out, are a "tragedy for American society."

It starts in the childhood of American males. When parents use the expression "he's all boy," what they mean is that he is aggressive, gets into trouble, or dirties himself. They never mean he is showing tenderness, emotion, or affection. "What parents are really telling their son is that a real man doesn't show his emotions and if he is a real man he won't allow his emotions to be expressed," says Dr. Peck. This is viewed as "a sign of femininity and undesirable for a male." The result is that the male child grows up to be tongue-tied like John Wayne or unfeeling like James Bond. Both types treat women "with an air of emotional detachment and independence." The playboy looks at sex as a packageable product; the woman in the process is reduced to a playboy accessory. The cowboy *feels*, all right—he loves his woman and his horse (or in the modern-day version, his car) equally, but the expression of such feeling would conflict with his image of masculinity.

What happens when either of the two characters marries can

[25]Quoted in the *San Francisco Chronicle*, September 20, 1970, p. 9.

easily be imagined. And the situation is not improved where a woman who has no special capacity for love is put in a position where she has nothing to do but love, as Vivian Gornick points out in the *Village Voice*. The result is that the modern American woman seeks to drive and dominate both her husband and her children. Says Miss Gornick:

> She displays an aberrated, aggressive ambition for her mate and her offspring, which can be explained only by the most vicious feelings toward the self. The reasons are obvious. The woman who must love for a living, the woman who has no self, no objective external reality to take her own measure by, no work to discipline her, no goal to provide the illusion of progress, no separate mental existence, is constitutionally incapable of the emotional distance that is one of the real requirements for love.[26]

Sexism does, indeed, have many and varied victims.

The Lost Potential

In his brilliant analysis of American democracy, *The Semi-Sovereign People*, E. E. Schattschneider concludes that the unused political potential in the United States could change the whole balance of power in the system. It is, in his comment, "sufficient to blow the United States off the face of the earth."[27]

What Schattschneider is referring to are the roughly 40 million adult citizens who do not vote in presidential elections (37.6 million in 1968). That is really "a stupendous segment of the nation" blocked out from the political system.[28] What makes it even more important is that their disfranchisement has been accomplished by extralegal means. It seems, in fact, to be voluntary. We have to worry about these 40 million adult Americans who seem to be "so unresponsive to the regime that they do not trouble to vote." To Schattschneider, their nonvoting makes a crucial difference—first, because "anything that looks like a rejection of the political

[26]Quoted in the *Sacramento Bee*, March 13, 1970, p. B3.
[27]E. E. Schattschneider, *The Semi-Sovereign People* (New York: Holt, Rinehart and Winston, 1969), p. 99.
[28]Schattschneider, p. 97.

system by so large a fraction of the population is a matter of great importance. Second, anything that looks like a limitation of the expanding universe of politics is certain to have great practical consequences."[29]

In the presidential election of 1968 there were more than 21 million women among the 37.5 million nonvoters. To get at the *practical* consequences flowing from their abstention from the polls, we have to do more than count numbers. We have to examine the social structure of the disfranchised, Schattschneider suggests. And if we are to get at the relationship of *sexist ideology* to the results obtained, we have to find the differences in turnout proportions between the sexes by geographical area, type of community, and level of education, for we know already that sex standards and sex-typing are the most rigid in the South, in village and rural areas, and among people on lower educational levels.

But first, who are the nonvoters generally? And how would our political system change if they were to suddenly invade it? As Schattschneider points out, "every study of the subject supports the conclusion that nonvoting is a characteristic of the poorest, least well-established, least educated stratum of the community."[30] We cannot, therefore, take it for granted that the 37.5 million or so abstainers would be divided along the conservative-liberal-radical spectrum in the same proportion as the 67.8 million who are now participants in the system. It is more likely they would line up behind programs and candidates that would improve and expand the welfare state, end poverty, and bring forth a greater measure of social justice and economic security for the common citizen. Self-interest is, after all, a strong and reasonably steady factor in voting behavior. "False consciousness" and the tendency to go with obvious public favorites may enter into and distort the picture somewhat,[31] but in general, one can argue as the late authority V.

---

[29]Schattschneider, p. 99

[30]Schattschneider, p. 105.

[31]It is, for instance, well established that members of the working class favor the Democratic party, looked to as the sponsor of welfare programs, while middle- and upper-class groups favor Republicans. See, for example, S. M. Lipset, *Political Man* (New York: Doubleday, 1959). On the other hand, a "psychological bandwagon effect," discovered in the elections of 1952 and 1956, where General Eisenhower was a heavy public favorite, indicates that on such occasions the general Democratic preference of nonvoters is likely to be unreliable. See Angus Campbell et al., "Voting Turnout," in Norman R. Lutbeg, ed., *Public Opinion and Public Policy* (Homewood, Ill.: Dorsey Press, 1968), pp. 46–58.

O. Key did, that "voters are not fools—in the large the electorate behaves about as rationally and responsibly as we should expect given the clarity of the alternatives presented to it and the character of the information available to it."[32] Schattschneider concurs: the present cleavages tend to freeze the stakes of politics at a point that has never involved the whole community. "The root of the problem of nonvoting is to be found in the way in which the alternatives in America politics are defined, the way in which issues get referred to the public, the scale of competition and organization, and above all *what* issues are developed."[33]

It is, of course, a two-way flow. Citizens stay away from the polls primarily because politics does not seem to relate to their needs. And politicians, on the other hand, refrain from developing and pursuing issues that do not seem to have much relevance to the citizens presently active in the political system. As a consequence, "a multitude of causes languish because the 40 million or so nonvoters do not support them at the polls." What would happen if they intervened staggers the imagination. "All political equations would be revised."[34]

So it is those on the bottom of the social order who stand to gain the most from an expansion of the popular base of political participation. To anyone who agrees with Schattschneider that a special sensitivity to *their* needs and experiences is one of the great moral claims of democracy as a system, it becomes vitally important to eradicate the causes for nonparticipation—to the extent, at least, that it leads to certain social issues being defined out of politics. The cause *we* are interested in, the ideology of sexism, appears to be responsible for the absence of more than 4.5 million potential votes in the last election, for this is the difference in turnout between men and women at that time. We need not for the moment touch on the problem of expanding the scope of the political system in general. Let us, then, look at the possible impact these 4.5 million votes might have on the political scene today.

To verify our hypothesis concerning the relationship between social structure and sexist ideology to nonvoting among women, let us take a closer look at the data. There may be, to be sure, a variety

[32]V. O. Key, *The Responsible Electorate* (Cambridge: Harvard University Press, 1966), p. 7.
[33]Schattschneider, *The Semi-Sovereign People*, p. 110.
[34]Schattschneider, pp. 110–11.

of reasons for women not going to the polls. Beyond the reasons that are common to both sexes, child-care responsibilities are the most likely obstacle, yet researchers found this to make little difference in voting turnout. Childless women in the South and childless women of grade-school education vote less frequently than men in the same categories. Also, this presumed barrier is not present for older women, yet sex differences in voting turnout do not diminish accordingly in this case either.[35]

TABLE 7.1   Relation of Sex, Education, and Region
to Political Involvement, 1952 and 1956 Elections

	Men			Women		
	Grade School	High School	College	Grade School	High School	College
Non-South						
High involvement	27%	36%	49%	19%	30%	46%
Medium involvement	36	45	41	34	46	46
Low involvement	37	19	10	47	24	8
	100%	100%	100%	100%	100%	100%
Number of cases	387	494	219	399	719	186
South						
High involvement	29%	33%	38%	14%	25%	57%
Medium involvement	32	39	49	33	41	35
Low involvement	39	28	13	53	34	8
	100%	100%	100%	100%	100%	100%
Number of cases	187	146	77	217	232	83

Source: Angus Campbell, Philip E. Converse, Warren E. Miller, and Donald E. Stokes, *The American Voter* (Ann Arbor, Mich.: Survey Research Center, University of Michigan, 1960), p. 490. Reprinted by permission of the Survey Research Center.

[35]Campbell et al., *The American Voter*, pp. 487–88.

As the University of Michigan's Survey Research Center's team found out, it is *where* women live and *how much education* they have absorbed that more than anything else influences their participation in politics. Table 7.1, showing some of the results of this study, points to some of these factors; Table 7.2 makes the picture even clearer. As pointed out earlier, it is in the areas where sex-typing generally is most rigid that the differences show up.

The conclusion drawn by the scholars responsible for this study, published as *The American Voter*, parallels our own conclusion. According to them, it is "vestigial sex roles" that make for the basic differences in the political participation of men and women,[36] "vestigial" because the granting of suffrage to women implies a shift in former role definitions, where the man was the political agent for the family unit and the woman was not to concern herself with politics. As we have seen, however, these vestiges of political patriarchy are too prominent and influential to be taken lightly. They would seem to be responsible for no less than 4.5 million votes lost to the nation in the presidential election of 1968, this being the number of women nonvoters over men nonvoters. Unless, of course, the cleavages among these nonparticipants were to correspond to those existing among the voters, this could make for a very different outcome in elections and very different outcomes in policy formulation and output by the officials elected.

TABLE 7.2   Average Differences in
Turnout Proportions of the Sexes, Non-South

Area	*Male-Female Gap*
Metropolitan	+ 5%
City and town	+ 20%
Village and rural	+ 28%

Source: Campbell, Converse, and Stokes, p. 487. Reprinted by permission of the Survey Research Center.

[36]Campbell et al., p. 484.

Let us remember that the 1968 election was decided with a small differential of popular votes in favor of the Republican presidential candidate. Let us also keep in mind that the nonvoters, *in particular* the women nonvoters, are by and large on the lower socioeconomic levels. Residence in rural areas and in the South and lower educational levels, primary factors in the explanation of greater ratios of nonvoting among women, are equally factors pointing to the likelihood of this group being on the bottom of the social barrel. Given, then, the usual preference for the Democratic party among citizens in the "out-groups" of society, it seems clear that the invasion of these 4.5 million women into the political system would at the very least have ensured the election of a Democratic administration. Approximately 60 percent of women nonvoters in the 1968 election did, in fact, declare their preference for the Democratic party, whereas only 20 percent in the same group chose the Republican party as their favorite.[37] The presence of George Wallace in this race would have made little difference; given the greater preference for peace candidates among women in general, the blatantly hawkish tone of his campaign did not appeal to many women. In fact, among those who voted for Wallace in 1968, women counted for less than one-third of the total support.[38] Insofar as the presidential election of 1968 is concerned, then, there is little doubt that *if* these 4.5 million "feminine" citizens had been able to overcome their inhibitions and prejudices to actually go to the polls, *their* vote would have won the day for the Democratic presidential candidate!

That in itself carries quite an impact on the political and social scene of America. The central position of the presidency in the system is, as noted earlier, recognized by everyone. Although the two major parties in recent decades have tended to come closer in programs and policies, the difference in emphasis on the need to eradicate poverty, to channel funds into higher education, and to support civil rights programs have emerged as significant, particularly in the first years of the Nixon administration. A Democratic administration would be honor-bound to try to bring the unemployment rate down, and equally, to continue programs aimed at aiding the "out-groups" in American society. With an influx of, say, at least 3 to 3.5 million supporters on the lower socioeconomic

[37]Survey Research Center, University of Michigan.
[38]Survey Research Center, University of Michigan.

levels, the liberals of the party would be in a stronger position to push the kind of policies traditionally favored by their sector. What that could mean, in the end, would be a genuine welfare state with a certain level of economic security, full medical care, and educational opportunities guaranteed to every citizen.

An expansion of the effective political community would quite simply mean new and greater emphasis on the options and alternatives that reflect the needs of the present nonparticipants. The impact of the newcomers should quickly make itself felt within the Republican party as well. If cleavages within the body of voters now active in the system do not change, this party, too, would have to move in the direction of liberalization in the socioeconomic sphere, if it is to win in future national elections. Registration is already in the favor of the Democrats; the margin of victory for Republican candidates is generally very small, and the Goldwater-Johnson contest in 1964 offered convincing evidence that even without the influx of several million new voters on lower socioeconomic levels, there is a decisive trend against the type of candidates and platforms that promise a halt or turning back of welfare programs now in existence. Barring intervening issues carrying great and unusual emotional loads, a true conservative cannot be elected on the national level at least.

Another important result to be obtained from the projected expansion of the effective electorate if sexist ideology were to lose its hold would be a gradual diminution in the now shocking dimension of the nonvoting sector of the American polity, both male and female, since new policies would better relate to their needs. Their current abstention reflects nothing so much as the fact that conflicts now familiar to American politics have little relevance for them. But as both parties go after the 4.5 million women voters who are now held back mainly by "vestigial" sex roles, they will have to, given the usual income and status of these women, raise issues and make proposals that bear on the fates of nonvoters of both sexes. As a consequence, a different organization of politics should ensue, bringing us closer to a nationalization of politics where "competing leaders and organizations devine the alternatives of public policy in such a way that the public can participate in the decision-making process."[39]

---

[39]Schattschneider, *The Semi-Sovereign People*, p. 141.

Such is Schattschneider's *operational* definition of democracy. We cannot think of a better one. Whether it fits the American system as now organized is quite another question. Even the most eloquent and perceptive defender of our political order, Robert Dahl, agrees that the rates of political participation that have been characteristic of this citizen body are "deplorably low."[40] An expansion in the scope of the political community is essential whatever one's conception of democracy. In our preferred order, there simply is no room for *a silenced majority.*

---

[40]Robert A. Dahl, "Further Reflections on the Elitist Theory of Democracy," *American Political Science Review* 2 (June 1966): 301.

eight

The Liberated Society
vision and strategies

What does woman want? Or—what does woman need?

At this point in time the two questions are likely to bring forth quite different responses. Given the impact and pervasiveness of sexist ideology, one cannot expect that the majority of American women will express any interest in changing the traditional role and place of woman in this society. But reformers and rebels have never waited for the masses to give approval for them to go ahead in their drive to free humans from their shackles. It would be a much sadder and poorer world, indeed, if they did. Instead, they allow normative ideals, a vision of a better future, and faith in the possibility of change to guide their action. And, at times, they have been proven right. It would be hard to argue—with *some* knowledge of human history—that either change or improvements in the human condition are impossible. Certainly, the "heroes of history" never heeded the advice of the pessimists. As single-minded as they were passionate, they forged ahead in their reformatory or revolutionary drives no matter how few their followers or how great the obstacles at the start. More often than not, history confirms the truth in the old maxim: "There is no stopping of an idea whose time has come."

So it may be with the new feminism in America. Since it is based on the belief that women are *humans* entitled to the same opportunities for self-expression as men, the question for the movement is *not* what women want as of the present, but *what women need* to become free and fully realized individuals. No false theories of woman's nature, no ideologically based view of her proper role in society, no artificial sex norms can be allowed to stand in the way of the human development of the female. Equality of education, equality of opportunity, equality of income, and status on a par with men are about the most basic and immediate demands of the new 'feminists. Beyond that, the true liberation of the American woman requires a society structured quite differently than America is right now. What is needed is a society where arrangements are made to ensure the realization and utilization of the potential of *every* human being, for there are too many men among us whose talents remain undeveloped, whose skills are not used, whose spirits are still twisted. To simply aspire to *their* current status and position, therefore, although it would imply a significant improvement in the lot of women, cannot in the long run satisfy the variety of needs and interests suppressed for thousands of years. Women have had to wait too long and male domination has been too complete for the reforms in question to accomplish the transformation of both life style and quality of life envisioned by most feminists. Their aspirations and needs will necessitate far-reaching and profound change, change that cannot help but free the men of America, as well. The liberation of women will mean—*must* mean—the liberation of men.

What It Could Be Like

Let us reflect on the character and qualities of a society where both sexes are allowed a full and free flowering of talents and a choice of work and life style that is in line with their temperament and desires. This would have to be a society where sex norms were concerned with maintaining the dignity of individuals and essential decency and sensitivity in a sexual union. No more. Each person could be herself or himself—emotional, rational, assertive, quiet, strong, or weak—without fear of violating sex standards and dangerously straying from the approved sex-typing. A young man might cry at movies, write poetry, dance ballet, or enjoy feeding and caring for a family without crushing the fears and doubts about his manhood now forced upon him by sexist ideology. A young woman might decide that she loves the rough and tumble of politics, the daring pursuit of, say, race-car-driving, or the serious and dedicated work of scientists, and she might freely be assertive, competitive, and dominant socially or at work, without the gnawing doubts and cruel put-downs now common for such "unfeminine" behavior. In their relationships with one another, people could equally transcend the stereotyping we know only too well. *She* might at times take the initiative for both social engagements and sexual encounters; he just possibly might enjoy being the one pursued, the more passive partner. More importantly, they could be companions and friends, not just husband and wife, not just sexual beings seeking from each other a hard-won gratification of both ego and physical desires. Creativity, sharing, and joy in a sexual union could be possible as both partners developed a clear concept of self and were free from the rigidities of current sex-typing and sex norms.

In such a society, the family could take a variety of forms. It is a fair bet that it will be with us for quite some time yet, but a relaxation in its role structure and experimentation with its form is bound to come. No longer need the only fully approved family unit be the one where father is the breadwinner, mother the housewife, and Mary and Joe the overprotected, TV-dazed little kids dividing their time between neighborhood school and cozy suburban homestead. There can instead be a variety of options for the activities and life style of all family members. In the family that stayed nuclear in form, the mother in our liberated society would have a chance to take on the work of her choice, and that would include, of course, the chance to stay on as a housewife. Only this time, her work would be socially valued, with the usual guarantees of time off, vacation, and pension upon retirement. If she decided to join the labor force outside, there would be attractive, secure, and well-staffed child-care centers available for the children. And when she came home, then, from her outside job, both she and the father— possibly the children, too—would share in the care and maintenance of family and home, freeing her to be a true companion and friend to all. The father, equally, would have more options available to him. He might choose to stay home or to experiment in a variety of occupations, secure in the knowledge that the financial responsibility was no longer his alone and that no one would ever question his manhood on the basis of his preference in work or social life.

But the nuclear family might no longer fill the needs of a good number of individuals. A communal arrangement or an extended family would offer to many a greater flexibility and freedom, without in any way diminishing the sense and experience of sharing and responsibility. Such experimental units are, in fact, quite in vogue today among groups of younger people. The possibilities here are exciting, but, unquestionably, present sexual mores get in the way of building the kind of commune that would free women from their stereotyped menial assignments—or from sexual exploitation. The answer is *not* the supersexed group life carried to nightmarish dimensions by the Charlie Manson "family." What is happening here is simply that a woman is expected to have sexual relations with any man who wants to, without regard to *her* inclinations and taste at the moment. Neither is the answer the kind of back-to-nature, "hip" communes where women still end up doing their "womanly" things and where the cleaning, scrubbing, and cooking are only more arduous, servile, and backbreaking than back in the much-suspected consumer culture. No, and emphatically no. In a liberated society such cultural throwbacks would get only the contempt and ridicule they deserve. For communes to be genuine communities, sharing of responsibilities, decisions, and pleasures would *not* take place in accordance with sex divisions.

The greatest advantage offered by an extended family is that children would be free from the sometimes suffocatingly close atmosphere of suburban home life and would learn to know and live with a variety of people of many ages, backgrounds, and personalities. The children would learn to take on responsibilities for themselves and others; egotism and a keen sense of possession would be discouraged, since trust and sharing are the qualities needed and fostered by such living arrangements. The greater and more varied exposure to other humans, the feeling of brotherhood and common purpose known to the best of such families, could not help but make children both happier and more humanly decent individuals. Responsiveness and responsibility would replace the dependence and selfishness found in many children subject to the excessive mothering of an omnipresent mother and the occasional, exasperated attention of a much-harassed father. We have, in fact, much evidence on hand that the children raised in the kibbutzes of Israel or in the child-care centers of Scandinavia and the Soviet Union are both mentally healthier than the majority of American children today.[1]

Joy could come back to marriage and interest be added to ongoing relationships when the union of man and woman implied an enlargement of the life experiences for both and not the sudden withdrawal and exclusive focus on home and marriage for her. A woman could seek a mate and eventually children only when she truly desired this experience. There would be no more social pressure and snickering contempt for the woman who did not marry. The relief for the man should be considerable; the groom who tries escape outside the church door is so common a figure in our folklore that it testifies to widespread resentment of the pressures and manipulation trapping *him* as well. Fatherhood, like motherhood, would be a question of free and thoughtful choice. Children would not be brought into the world because of infantile fantasies about cute, cuddly babies bringing feminine fulfillment or adding decor to the home scene. Nor would they be fathered because of deep-rooted insecurities and half-crazed drives to prove one's masculinity or add status through the acquisition of offspring. In our liberated society, the educational experiences and the mass culture would not force on men and women such conflicting needs and divisive experiences. Both would be reared as individuals, with talents and temperaments specific to the *person*, not to the *sex*; and both would learn self-reliance, responsibility, and self-respect as they grew and developed. Cooperation, spiritual union, excitement in sexual relations could then take the place of debilitating suspicions and the terrible hostility now so familiar between the sexes. Both everyday behavior and common and highbrow culture testify to the presence of latent but intense sexual resentments and "impotent rage," to use Betty Friedan's term. It is remarkable, as she has

[1]See, for example, the overview of several studies in David Rapaport, "The Study of Kibbutz Education and Its Bearing on the Theory of Development," *American Journal of Orthopsychiatry* 28 (1958): 587–99; Bruno Bettelheim, "Growing Up Female," *Harper's*, October 1962; Jane Whitbreak, "A New Way to Raise Kids," *Look*, February 24, 1970, pp. 64–68; Urie Brontenbreuner, *Two Worlds of Childhood* (New York: Russel Sage Foundation, 1970); and the discussion in Alice S. Rossi, "Inequality between the Sexes," in R. J. Lifton, ed., *The Woman in America* (Boston: Houghton Mifflin, 1964), pp. 106–19.

pointed out, that all a stand-up comedian has to do to start his audience tittering and guffawing is to come out on stage and say two words: "My wife. . . ."[2] Yet as women are liberated the sex war in America *can* come to an end, as indeed it *must* before it does further damage to relationships and the quality of social and political life in general.

The Institutional Transformation

Concretely, what such a society demands is a variety of institutional innovations and a complete reordering of economic priorities. The current platforms of women's rights groups offer a good *start*, but *no more than that*, in policy proposals called for to bring about a sexually liberated society. The demands by now include equal pay and equal opportunities, paid maternity leaves with guarantees for women to return to their jobs, well-staffed and sound child-care centers in the communities or at the places of employment, pensions and severance pay for housewives, and an end to all discriminatory practices both on the job and in public accommodations, to be ensured, preferably, by the enactment of the Equal Rights Amendment. To this list must be added the very important request that the image of women in the mass media and in children's textbooks be changed. Women must be portrayed as something other and something more than brainless sexpots or possessive and spiritually diminished house slaves.

Can even these demands be accommodated within the present political and economic structures? To some extent, yes; in some respects, no. They will, in the first place, require far greater public expenditures than are now afforded social programs in this society. On the other hand, child-care centers, housewives' pensions, and equal-pay arrangements are all policies already in effect in a number of societies with a proportionately far lower gross national product than we have in the United States. The Soviet Union and the socialist countries in general, and with a few exceptions, West Germany, the Scandinavian countries, and England, are all

[2]Speech delivered at Sacramento State College, October 8, 1970.

pledged to and on the way to implementing such programs, if they are not already in full operation.[3]

Given these latter examples, it is clear that the capitalist system need not be totally transformed in order to introduce the reforms in question. Neither will the present feminist demands impose impossible burdens on the economy. They will, however, require a substantial reshuffling of budgetary expenditures, as well as the acceptance of new tasks of social responsibility on the part of industry and institutions of higher education. Child-care centers at the place of work or study, paid maternal leaves, and equal pay are innovations that will not come cheaply to the employers and institutions with whom women are involved today. For the small-scale ones, governmental subsidies may be necessary. But for the rest, both the general rate of profits taken in yearly and the very great earnings derived over the years from sex discrimination should make sufficient provisions for the institution of these reforms.

A warning must be issued at this point, lest it be thought that the road ahead will be an *easy* one to travel. The programs outlined will not be adopted by the mere appeal to the common sense and humanitarian instincts of the elites. *Political pressures* will have to be applied at all points. Confrontation politics may still have its uses at certain points, but these will have to be combined with the thrust of organized groups of women *and* the allies of women working for the reforms needed.

It may be a drawn-out and tiresome process, unless women behind the feminist program succeed in doing what no other outgroup in American society has done so far: organizing across class, race, and ethnic lines. A coalition will have to be formed and a political force created strong enough *either* to force upon the power wielders all the major changes required *or* to put into power individuals and groups committed to the enactment of the essential reform package. It should be obvious after reviewing the data in the earlier part of the book that the greatest, most crying needs

[3]Norway, Denmark, and England have yet to enact legislation for housewives' pensions or severance pay. In the Scandinavian countries and West Germany, abortion is free, that is, it is paid for through the system of government-insured medical care, but cannot be had at the request of the mother-to-be. Doctors have to agree that abortion is socially or medically necessary.

among women are to be found among working-class women, black and white, and among women who are alone in raising their families. Given the great numbers of women in these groups, at least 25 million in the job market in the mid-seventies, it is clear that *could* they be reached by the new feminist consciousness and brought around to actively support the feminist program, the movement would be formidable, indeed, in the political arena as well as on the sociocultural scene.

The problems in creating such a coalition will be discussed shortly, but for now it must be emphasized that tactics will have to be flexible and diversified in dealing with business elites, the media, the educational establishment, and labor unions. In regard to the first two, the consumer boycott together with sharply focused public critiques and legal challenges can be supremely effective as the movement comes to encompass larger numbers. Few businesses, including the media, can afford the damage to their prestige and the consequent financial loss involved in the persistent alienation of a substantial group of citizens. As selected products or companies are singled out for punishment because of refusals to correct either inequities toward women workers or media messages doing insult or injury to women, the lesson should be rather quickly learned by others. Few are invulnerable, especially not as the weapon of consumer boycott comes into use. The threat of cutoffs in government contracts or subsidies is also to be taken very seriously by a great many—provided, of course, that women exert greater pressure upon government to make a reality of Affirmative Action programs.[4]

Ultimately, the government must be made the ally of women in their quest for equality and liberation. Beyond adopting and implementing legislation to insure equity and opportunities for women in education and on the job market, it is to governmental sources one will have to look for the financing of a major portion of the feminist program. Housewives' pensions, the reeducation of women necessary to create a true measure of equality of opportunity, as well as the rewriting of public-school textbooks and the initia-

[4]A review article from August 1974 draws the following conclusion: "The general feeling among many women leaders, affirmative action officers and some administrators is that affirmative action is not working." Cheryl M. Fields, "Affirmative Action: 4 years After," *Chronicle of Higher Education*, August 5, 1974, p. 7.

tion of course programs on women all have to be funded by government on various levels. The problem of *how* to make government the ally in this enterprise is basically that of how to awaken the political consciousness of women and to create the conditions conducive to a political thrust. A variety of examples from the past suggest that forceful pressure groups, strong electoral minorities, or—as in this case—a potential electoral majority can force surprising changes upon both "kingmakers" and lawmakers in a democracy. We shall discuss the problem of creating political awareness at some length later in this chapter. Before we go on, however, the *money question* has to be attended to. Quite simply, where is the necessary money going to come from, given the already excessive demands on the budget, both on the federal and state level, and the very heavy tax burdens imposed on the average citizen today?

There is no holy order, no unconquerable spirit that decrees that our *budgetary priorities* shall continue to be what they are at present. Women can and will have to question the propriety of having 70 percent of federal budgetary outlays go to "defense needs." It is a fair bet that they will be joined in making that challenge by a sizable number of men. With the war in Southeast Asia at an end and the reported need for American troops in Europe and elsewhere less and less convincing, chances appear quite good for a reordering of governmental priorities, a reordering essential for even the minimal demands of feminists to be met. It will, of course, require political action—by and on behalf of women and other "outgroups" in American society. This has already started. The present plight of large numbers of workers and defense experts suddenly left without jobs, is likely, if anything, to add momentum to the drive for deemphasis on defense and reemphasis on social programs.

The point to be made here is: *it can be done*. The feminist program, as outlined here, can be enacted without too much straining or radical transformation of the present economic structures. What we have talked about so far are reforms and innovations common to democratic welfare states as well as socialist states; and what has happened in the former confirms the judgment of many economists that the capitalist order is more flexible and durable than earlier suspected. An overthrow of the system is as unlikely as it is unnecessary for the eradication of the most overt of institutionally sanctioned sexist behavior. What will be required, however, is a serious modification toward a more mixed economy, where the government takes on new responsibilities and new authority vis-à-vis corporate elites and where women and their allies are in the position vis-à-vis government of demanding far greater accountability and responsiveness to their needs.

What makes such changes possible and even likely in our time are a few prominent developments of a social, political, and economic nature that tend to converge and thereby to confirm the historic invincibility of the feminist idea in this period. Economically, we have come to the point in our society where the problem is no longer to increase production generally in order to create *new* surplus capital for the upgrading of life among the present underprivileged group. For that, all we need is a more fair and equitable distributive system and a rechanneling of expenditures on the governmental level. Our productive apparatus is, in fact, capable of putting out all the goods necessary to ensure the material well-being of every American alive, and then with some surplus to spare. Ordinarily—that is, in peacetime—our productive apparatus generally operates at about 60 percent capacity, for the simple reason that not enough income has been generated among American consumers to avail themselves of the products and inventions the market so easily may offer. This is not to suggest that what we need in this country is more consumerism among those already affluent. We may, on the contrary, need less—a shift in emphasis as to socially valued goods among these groups is highly desirable from the point of view of anyone concerned with human and not just materialistic values. We do, however, have among us about 45 million people living in poverty or in "near"-poverty.[5] This one-fourth to one-fifth of our nation can surely use more and better housing, clothing, and nutrition, all of which can be made available to them by merely utilizing the presently unused portion of our productive apparatus. Beyond that, we can *all* use better schools, more hospitals, improved recreation facilities, cleaner air and water.

What is so striking about this great accumulation of pressing

[5]This is the estimate of economists reported in Kenneth Dolbeare and Murray Edelman, *American Politics: Power, Policy, and Change* (New York: Markham, 1974), p. 34.

public needs is that they occur at a time when the problem for our manufacturers is not the ability to expand production facilities and rates, but rather *where* to channel surplus capital and *how* to prevent constriction due to the inability of the consuming public to absorb what they can offer. If part of that surplus capital were redirected to the public in the form of a greater share of the profits to the employees and to the public coffers for the purpose of meeting social needs, then both our corporate economy and the public sector could flourish. Clearly, the expansion required to meet these needs cannot now come in the defense sector. Since this industry is already overdeveloped, technological trends and innovations have meant that even the most extravagant new programs, such as space exploration, will employ relatively few of the best trained and most highly educated. The employment picture generally will not improve; the great public expenditures will not be "spread around." And it is that "spreading around" that we now have an imperative need for.

Consequently, as these facts become known and are absorbed by politically active groups among the public, pressures may be applied toward government to make the necessary changes in both the taxation system and the budget to improve our public life and our economy. Corporation elites will resist, to be sure, since the changes suggested will cut into their overall rate of profits and partially into their rights to make decisions not in line with public needs. In the long run, however, it is in their own enlightened self-interest to go along with such reforms—as corporation elites in Western Europe have come to discover, a mixed economy and expanded welfare state are both inevitable and beneficial for their own overall interests.

This is why the economic part of feminist demands can and will be met, provided there is the kind of political awakening and thrust always needed to get democratic government off a dead end and start it moving in new directions. Socially and politically, the time is ripe as well for activists in the feminist and progressive camps to gain in their advances—socially because the myth of "capitalism for the workers" is gradually being exposed as the sham it is, with the lack of job security and the vagaries of the stock market most often hitting the little guy, as dramatically evidenced in recent years; socially also because of the growing awareness of a multitude of social needs and the increasing tendency to look to government to meet them; politically because the prominent egalitarian strain in American political thought makes for a likely acceptance of the moral basis for the feminist claims; and politically also because the ground has been prepared, so to speak, for reformers' drives and activists' thrusts by the multitude of radical challenges hurled at "the establishment" in recent years.

Beyond all this, beyond the envisioned enactment of the present feminist program, it must again be recognized that *further reforms* are required for a decent and creative life to be possible for all Americans. The greater infusion of women in the work force, for example, will necessitate fewer work hours daily or a shorter work week for all. Housing patterns may have to be changed as it becomes more common for both parents to work: the isolation and heavy commuting connected with suburbia should be replaced with communities where work, social activities, and family life can be more easily and pleasurably integrated. Vacations must be extended for both parents. Both family and personal needs and contemporary practices call for an urgent revision of the current American vacation pattern. (Many technologically advanced societies offer all workers one month of paid vacation yearly, none offer less than three weeks.) If abortion laws are to be liberalized and abortions essentially financed through government agencies, medical care for both sexes is due for a similar general reorganization. And if women are to be given the chance to get all the educational and occupational opportunities their talents and efforts prove them to be suited for, then men too require the same for themselves. The educational apparatus, consequently, will have to be expanded, with access and finances guaranteed to everyone qualified. The job market, too, will require expansion, with a far greater emphasis on the utilization of all talents and much more room for experimentation.

It may be that the enactment of far-reaching programs such as these require in the end not just a modification, but a whole transformation of the present economic structure. But then we are greatly aided by the fact that both our ethical principles and industrial needs press precisely toward a greater egalitarianism. It is a major theme both in the American creed and in Western philosophy and ethics generally that all humans have a right to an equal opportunity. That can only mean, in the context of our time, that as children and young people they be provided with *all* they need to *learn* and to *develop*—which includes not only schooling, but also decent housing, nutrition, and health care. It also means, as William J. Goode points out, that talent may be found in any segment of the society and that when education transforms talent into skill, this should be put to use.[6]

The time has come, then, for the feminist ideas, for the feminist program and all that it implies to sweep to the forefront and gradually win acceptance—not just by women, but by everyone with an interest in the future of this nation.

The Struggle Ahead

The movement, it is said, has come of age. Meaning, as is often reported, that the original impetus, the enthusiasm and will to engage in radical confrontations among new-found feminists, has dissipated. At the same time, however, women's rights organizations have multiplied and are stronger than ever in terms of numbers; significant victories have been won in the legislative and legal fields for women, and the last few years have brought a whole explosion of women's studies programs and courses in American colleges together with the emergence of a highly successful mass magazine expressly committed to the feminist perspective and cause.[7]

This is but part of the "mushroom effect" of the movement, as a directory of 1970 termed it. In the late seventies women's groups with a focus on consciousness raising, assertiveness training, rape prevention, support through a variety of crises, and, of course, political action number in the several thousands throughout the

[6]William J. Goodie, *World Revolution and Family Patterns* (Englewood Cliffs, N.J.: Prentice-Hall, 1964).

[7]As of 1975, NOW claimed 55,000 members and NWPC (National Women's Political Caucus) had 37,000 names on their mailing lists; other organizations of note, such as Women's Equity Action League (WEAL) and Women's Lobby Inc., involved several thousands more women. Legislative victories are referred to in Chapters 2 and 3 of this book. Women's studies programs numbered eighty-two and women's studies courses two thousand in 1973. *Ms.* magazine reached a circulation of well over 1 million in 1975.

country. It must also be remembered that this is not a movement one necessarily *joins*, as Robin Morgan pointed out years ago:

> The Women's Liberation Movement exists where three or four friends or neighbors decide to meet regularly over coffee and talk about their personal lives. It also exists in the cells of women jails, on the welfare lines, in the supermarket, the convent, the farm, the street-corner, the old ladies' home, the kitchen, the steno pool, the bed. It exists in your mind and in the personal and political insights that you can contribute to change and help its growth.[8]

What is overlooked, as outside observers of "Women's Lib" make their usual sarcastic comments, is that the movement has succeeded remarkably well in raising the consciousness of a majority of women in the United States. Frustrated and stymied as the activists may feel at times in terms of achieving more than consciousness, moving beyond tokenism, they can still take heart and courage from the very real changes in opinions and attitudes that are reliably recorded among American women in these last few years.

In the early polls testing American women's views and reactions to the new stirrings, it was reported—with glib satisfaction—that they were in the majority happy and satisfied with their "womanly" roles and that they disapproved of "Women's Liberation."[9] Certain glaring inconsistencies in these findings were perceived, however. To quote, for instance, from pollster Louis Harris: "The American woman says she is sexually fulfilled, but two out of five think men are only interested in their own sexual gratification. And while two out of three think a man is essential for a woman's happiness, a *majority* say that most men don't respect their opinions, see them as mindless sex objects and find it necessary for their egos to keep women down."[10]

In the spring of 1973 the Roper Poll found, again, that only a minority of American women felt that they were discriminated against (24 percent). Note, however, that at the same time 89 percent agreed that women *should* have equal job opportunities with men, 61 percent that there *should* be free or low-cost child-care

---

[8]Robin Morgan, *Sisterhood Is Powerful* (New York: Vintage, 1970), p. xxxvi.
[9]See, for example, the Roper Polls and the Gallup Polls of 1970. (Italics added.)
[10]Quoted in the *San Francisco Chronicle*, March 23, 1973, p. 16.

centers for working mothers, and 74 percent that women *should* have equal pay with men.[11]

The surveys up to that point indicated strongly that the major goals—as well as some of the key complaints—of the Women's Liberation movement enjoyed widespread approval among American women. And significantly, when the term *women's rights groups* rather than *Women's Liberation* is used in polls, the measure of approval is much higher. In April 1973, the Harris Poll found 56 percent of the public to have great respect for "women's rights groups"![12]

By 1974 we find public opinion in general backing the goals of feminism, with very strong support found in the younger generation, particularly among those in college or with a college education. The Virginia Slims American Women's Opinion Poll, conducted by the Roper organization, reports 57 percent among women respondents in favor of efforts to *strengthen* or *change* women's status in society, with only 25 percent opposed. In 1970, the reports showed only 40 percent in favor and 42 percent opposed to these same efforts.[13] A majority of women—and men, too—feel that women are discriminated against when it comes to getting better-paying jobs and in obtaining credit.[14]

It is clear through this as well as other surveys that the greatest discontent with women's fulfillment possibilities is found among women under thirty.[15] There appears to be very little chance that women from now on will settle for the bleak and confining "feminine" world that sexist ideology would proscribe for them. For those who have been touched by the ideas and aspirations of feminism—and they number now in the millions—there is no turning back.

The time of confrontation politics may have passed and the struggle ahead will seem less dramatic. It will not, however, require any less energy or dedication. For as any review of the actual versus

[11]Roper Poll, April 1973.

[12]Quoted in the *Sacramento Bee,* June 4, 1973, p. 11.

[13]*The Virginia Slims American Women's Opinion Poll,* a study conducted by the Roper Organization (1974) 3:4–7.

[14]*Virginia Slims Poll,* 3:4–7.

[15]*Virginia Slims Poll,* 3: 4–7. See also a recent study by Daniel Yankelovich, reported in *New York Times,* May 22, 1974, p. 43.

the apparent changes in the status of women will show, it takes more than the passage of new legislation or executive orders to change something as fundamental and all-pervasive as sexism in our society. The very real advances obtained by women in these areas still have not resulted in anything but token improvements, as we have seen; the mass of women, *working* women in the United States, are as disadvantaged and subject to economic hardship as they were before the advent of Women's Liberation.

This is surely the greatest shortcoming of the movement so far: it has not succeeded in establishing itself and organizing women of the working class. A beginning has been made with the creation of CLUW, the Coalition of Labor Union Women; but the major organizations, like NOW, retain their middle-class character and have yet to launch any drive to bring into their folds the millions of women living at or near the poverty level. It should be recognized, at the same time, that *any* movement in this society is likely to start with the better-educated groups, with people not totally weighed down by the struggle for survival; NOW, WEAL, NWPC, and so forth are simply no exceptions to that rule. But if the movement is to go beyond a predictable and threatened dead end—as it did with the passage of the Nineteenth Amendment—it will have to address itself to broad socioeconomic issues that will find response and be of relevance to *all* working women and to members of other "out-groups" in America as well. Unemployment, inflation, working conditions and pay, child care, pensions, and health care are the real and compelling issues of the middle and late seventies—issues in which *women* have the greatest stake. For we know already that women are the first and most frequent victims of economic dislocations and basic, persistent inequities in our economic system.

Converts will come as women demonstrate their seriousness and get their messages through to the public. It is important that leaders in the movement keep in mind the need not to step too far ahead of the main body of citizens. Antifamily, hate-male campaigns are strictly nonproductive both on the political and, in the long run, on the personal level. Although bold maneuvers, inventive campaigns, and dramatic challenges will have to be used to get the attention of the media, the tactics must be directed at *more* than that. They must be aimed at drawing to the movement *new* recruits and making possible the coalition with other "out-groups."

Women have causes in common both with other minorities and with blue-collar, technical, and salespersons in general, as shown in earlier chapters. What is interesting here is that neither the minorities nor the groups of workers we are talking about can by themselves obtain a majority coalition. But if they are joined with a substantial group of women, newly conscious of their rights and needs, the possibility for such a coalition wielding real power is by no means remote. What has plagued the civil rights movement in recent years is the seeming impossibility of going beyond the advances made for blacks with a promising culture and educational background. The bulk of black people are very little better off, socially and economically, than they were a decade ago, but the movement is unable to get off its present dead center until it can join in mass action to bring about thorough systemwide change. The situation is or will be the same for other minorities. Confrontation can bring about the modifications and improvements necessary to co-opt the activists and pacify rebelling groups, but for the government to transform itself to bring the present "out-groups" fully into the system, socially and economically, politicians will have to be shown the gradual but certain build-up of a voting majority.

A new political awakening is called for among the activists at this time: none of the rebelling groups can gain their aims without allies. Any broad strategy for change requires cooperation with carefully selected groups in and out of power. Well-defined group interests are essential to the process; the forceful and effective presentation of these in the public arena and by use of the mass media cannot help but draw new followers. As social ferments continue, other "out-groups" will go through a political awakening and before long the so-called silent majority, meaning the status quo–oriented and presumably content bloc of voters hitherto dominating the political scene, will be reduced to a minority. It is not this group, but the *silenced majority* that we have to worry about. The resurrection of democratic politics and the creation of social democracy in the United States require that they now prepare for an invasion into the system.

Whether feminists and their allies in the end choose to make use of the present party structure or to create a new one will depend on developments in the near future. Chances are that as the movement grows in numbers and proves itself capable of effective political organizing, politicians within both major parties will soon be on the scene trying to woo the members to their side by promises of support for their program. The danger of co-optation is ever-present and, for women, it carries with it a very special risk. The tendency of men to take over and dominate any group made up mainly of women and the inclination so long inbred in women to accept this practice have to be confronted and stopped in every instance. Women have to come into their own, have to discover their abilities and learn to take direction of their own fates without the supervision and guidance of men. "Cooperation, yes—co-optation, no" must be a rallying cry throughout the movement, if women are to transform their self-concepts and gain the self-respect they are so desperately in need of.

"Scratch a woman, and you will find a feminist!" comments Aileen Hernandez, 1970 president of NOW, meaning that any woman made to reflect on her own oppression will end up *as* angry and *as* set on change as are the activists of the movement. That is, indeed, the greatest hope for all who want to see the liberated society come about. If the "impotent rage" of American women can be changed to controlled anger and firm resolve, there will be no stopping of the feminist rebellion. Among those who find that a somewhat frightening prospect, let it be remembered that *a democracy ought not to fear its majority.*

Appendix 1

America, Gunnar Myrdal points out, has a more explicit political creed than any other Western nation. In the first chapter of *An American Dilemma*,[1] his now-classic study of the race problem of this country, Myrdal shows how all vehicles of communication are mobilized to indoctrinate every American with the principles in this American system of ideals. The "American creed" is taught in the schools, preached from the pulpits, announced by judges in their decisions. Editorials, articles, and public addresses all reflect the same idealism, and even oppressed minorities, like black Americans, share in the creed, pleading with it for their rights and even half-believing that it actually guides America. There is also some evidence, as shown in Chapter 7 of this book, that women hold to this creed more firmly and have greater faith in its guiding role than do men.

The ideals expressed in this creed are quite simply those of the dignity of the individual, fundamental equality, and certain inalienable rights to freedom, justice, and fair opportunity. These are the very principles written into the Declaration of Independence, the Preamble to the Constitution, the Bill of Rights, and the constitutions of the states. Myrdal's achievement in writing *An American Dilemma* lies not least in his demonstrating how these ideals are active realities, forming by themselves a dominant social trend.

[1]Gunnar Myrdal, *An American Dilemma: The Negro Problem and Modern Democracy* (New York: Harper & Brothers, 1942), p. 22.

While Americans do not live up to the creed in practice, sins against it are, on the other hand, loudly and incessantly proclaimed and lamented. It is the moral tension between ideals and practice regarding the treatment of black citizens particularly that Myrdal refers to as *the* American dilemma. The American creed is expressive and definite in all respects of importance for the race problem, according to his findings, and from the point of view of anyone sharing in that creed, "the status accorded the Negro in America represents nothing more and nothing less than a century-long lag in public morals."

The status of women in the contemporary United States must equally be seen as presenting a moral as well as a political dilemma to Americans. In this case, as well as in the case of black citizens, we are dealing with a national problem that cuts sharply through the whole body politic. And for us, just as for Myrdal, "no other set of valuations could serve as adequately as the norm for an incisive formulation of our value premises as can the American Creed."[2] It is so widely accepted, has such authority, and is so important as a real social trend that it is acceptable to use it as an "instrumental norm" for research. For, as Myrdal so convincingly demonstrates, the final solution to the value problem in social sciences generally must be to introduce human valuations openly and rationally into theoretical and practical research to give such research direction and purpose. At the same time, the value premises must be tested as to the relevance and significance in the society studied.

This latter task has already been admirably performed by Mrydal, and the historical records of the civil rights movement since the early sixties gives ample evidence for his earlier finding that the American creed is itself part of the social reality, being constantly called on by oppressed minorities fighting for their rights within this system. It should be added, however, that the ideals referred to here are not just American, but Western. They have found their most express articulation in this country, but they are, in essence, nothing but the humane ideals that have matured over the centuries in Western civilization generally.

---

[2] Gunnar Myrdal, *Value in Social Theory: A Selection of Essays on Methodology* (New York: Harper & Brothers, 1958), p. 68.

Appendix 2

The concept of class varies as widely as do theories of class and, as two authorities on the subject have conceded,[1] the discussions concerning the term are often academic substitutes for a real conflict over political orientations. The term *class* was initially used to simply distinguish social strata by their rank or wealth, but in the nineteenth century it emerged as an analytical category which has meaning only in the context of a theory of class. According to Karl Marx's model of class analysis, it is not permissible to interchangeably use the terms *class, stratum, rank,* and *position.* Except for *class,* these terms refer merely to groupings of people who occupy similar positions on a hierarchical scale in respect to such characteristics as income, prestige, and style of life; they are therefore nothing but descriptive categories. Marx's concept of class, on the other hand, contains a view of interest groups emerging from certain structural conditions that are subject to modification and change through the conflict between these same groups. Marx differs from former stratification analysts—and from present-day functionalists—in his insistence that the nature of the distributive system, and thereby the existence of classes, is determined by the productive system. As the productive system changes, the distributive system responds, but it is the classes that are the basic units in this process of evolution. To Marx it is class conflict which brings about the institutional

[1]S. M. Lipset and Reinhard Bendix, "Social Status and Social Structure," *British Journal of Sociology* 11 (1951).

changes required for progress to take place. For a comprehensive and insightful discussion of theories of class, with a particular emphasis on Marx, see Ralf Dahrendorf, *Class and Class Conflict in Industrial Society* (Stanford, Calif.: Stanford University Press, 1959).

In this study, the distinction between stratum and class is accepted, though it is left as an open question whether women on their own constitute merely a different stratum, or whether there are, in fact, such distinct structural factors in operation as to warrant use of the concept of class in regard to working women. In that case, the concept of "under class" may indeed be the most appropriate one, signifying that members of this grouping are not just inferior in terms of their share of income status, and power, but are generally viewed as subjects by members of the male master class.

It has been suggested that the special and highly disadvantaged position of women in the stratification system makes applicable the designation of *caste,* a closed social grouping into which a person is born and required to stay for life. The rank or social position of a caste member cannot be changed through personal qualities or achievement.[2] Undeniably, there are facts which tend to show the existence of a caste system in regard to women, yet at this point in time it appears too extreme an explanation. There are too many exceptions to the rule, too many "loophole women"[3] for us to take seriously the suggestion that we are here confronted with the most rigid of stratification systems in existence.

[2]For a thorough discussion of caste systems and other forms of stratification, see Gerhard Lenski, *Power and Privilege: A Theory of Social Stratification* (New York: McGraw-Hill, 1966).

[3]Caroline Bird, *Born Female* (New York: Pocket Books, 1969).

Index

Index

F